A Cry of Every
Woman's
Heart...

to be Loved

Deborah Cohen

ISBN:9781503079182

Printed in the USA

Cover design by Lynnette Bonner – www.indiecoverdesign.com
Edited by Teresa Sarros

For more information, visit: www.declaringzion.com
or contact Deborah at: declaringzion@yahoo.com

Other Titles by the Author:

The Biblical Essence of Wine, To Life... L'Chaim!
by Deborah Cohen

The Ninja and The Pastor
by Noam and Deborah Cohen

Contents

Preface

Now that the book has been finished and stuffed in a drawer for a few years, I understand the reason for the long delay in finally getting it printed. Unbeknownst to me at the time, my life was about to be radically changed, beyond anything I could have imagined, including a complete change of geography. However, the details of those years are for another book!

To be quite honest with you, the readers, looking back at the journey of trust I had to walk with the Lord, I now see that all thirteen women in this book have more than bits and pieces of myself in them. When I wrote these stories, I had no idea that I was interpreting what my own heart has said at different times in my life. The gift of writing has taught me that the words which flow through the fingers come from the heart, at least in my case. Maybe not many authors will admit this, and maybe it means I am too transparent, but this is who I am.

One thing is sure, however: I am not the only woman who loves the Lord who has had these feelings within. Countless conversations with other Christian women confirm that they, too, have the same need to know love and to feel that they are loved, whether by a husband, friend, or – as in this book – the Lord Himself. I pray and believe that my sisters who read this book will begin to see how much the Lord loves each and every one of us. He has created all women to be loved from the inside out.

As my life has taken its course, it has included valleys of despair, brokenness, failure, disappointment, and loneliness. But

He has always been there with me and has never left me. Human failure will always be a part of how we measure ourselves. But the Lord continually says, "Take My hand, and I will lead you through the highs and the lows. And even in the lows, I will be with you and never leave you nor forsake you."

The Lord is our all in all! He is every woman's dream come true. He is every woman's knight in shining armor. He is the answer to "A Cry of Every Woman's Heart…to be Loved."

Introduction:

The author's thoughts on "A Cry of Every Woman's Heart... to be Loved"

The cry of every woman's heart is to be loved. Whether she lived 2,000 years ago or today in the 21st century, the cry is the same. The year we were born, the surroundings in which we live, the amount of money we have, the number of family and friends who are a part of our lives, our outward appearance, whether we are short or tall – have no significance to the inner desire of a woman's heart to be loved. The women in this book wore robes that were perfectly in style for their time. You who are reading this book are probably in a style that is appropriate for this time. We can seem to "have it all" to those who measure happiness by abundance, but our hearts can be totally empty of the most required element to live – and that is to be loved. Whether we live in North America, South America, Africa, Asia, Australia, Europe, or Antarctica, women everywhere need to know that there is a Savior who loves us and that His plan of life for us is to be fulfilled as women who know they are loved.

There are so many wonderful stories in the Bible of Yeshua's love for the "other half" of the Kingdom, and we are called "woman." He showed respect to women and honored many by bringing attention to their sensitivity and ability to see through the circumstances around them to find Him.

We have down played the Book of Song of Songs because we have been taught that it is too much to handle; it is too personal. Or even worse, some just ignore it completely and figure if nobody talks about it, then it doesn't exist. Well, for us women it does exist, and it is a love story – not only between the Messiah and His soon-to-be bride, but it is a love story between a man and a woman. We were created not only to love and be loved by the Lord, but also to be loved by a man.

In my heart, I believe that the love story we read in the Bible should be a love story demonstrated and manifested here on this earth by a husband and wife. I believe that Yeshua opened the Garden of Eden to fulfill what He had purposed in the beginning for Adam and Eve before the fall. They were to be our example of a love story between a man and a woman.

The Lord is so good to us in our simple-minded ways that He brings forth love stories throughout the Word of God. When I think of Boaz and Ruth, I realize that God intends our lives to be a love story. That when His spirit brings two people together to complete each other, the love story of their lives does not end, lasting even to the season of sitting on park benches, still holding hands in their later years. I always stop and tell such couples how beautiful they are, and then praise the man for being a wonderful husband who brings a smile to his wife's face.

You who married the man of your dreams and remember the moment when the Lord revealed him to you, but feel unloved in your life now, go back to the Garden where he first saw you and you saw him and you knew the Spirit of God was there. Remind each other of the Garden of Delight. We can all tell when two people are in love, just as we can all tell when a person is in love with Yeshua. It is just obvious, and there is no hiding it. The world sees it and longs for it. That is why God created man and woman to become one, not just in the physical sense, but to be in love and to be completed by that other person. Just as Yeshua wants and desires us, so we want and desire to see Him and to be with Him. Two people in love are the most beautiful portrayal of Yeshua's love for us.

Now, to the single women of the Kingdom of God who live in the Garden of Eden, there is an Adam for you who is looking for his missing rib. Remember, the Garden is big! You are the only, exact, perfectly-matched rib that will fit into the man God perfectly created for you, which was purposed from the beginning of time. Think about how special you are! It just takes a time of trusting and waiting in God's presence for this husband-to-be to find you in the Garden, but he will. Stay in God's presence, rejoice in His goodness towards you, remain in perfect peace though the seasons come and go, and he will find you.

I have found myself saying to single women, "Do you have a desire to get married?" Their answer is "Yes." And then I go on to say, "Who put that desire in your heart – you or the Lord himself?" It always brings them to the conclusion that all desires come from Him if you walk in His presence and seek His ways. "Delight yourself in the Lord, and He will give you the desires of YOUR heart." Psalm 37:4 (NASB)

A woman longs to feel secure and protected by the one she is in love with and to know in her heart that he will never look at another. Again, it is the same between Yeshua and His bride. A bride wants to know that when she walks down that aisle, even with a pimple on her face, she is, in her soon-to-be husband's eyes, the most beautiful woman in the world. I admire King Solomon who wrote his story of love with the Shulamite woman. They both spoke freely of the physical attraction to each other. How freeing and intimate for both of them. The Lord not only gave us a spirit and a soul, but also a body to be loved by the other.

I want to encourage women everywhere to hold on to your dreams and desires of being loved. Yes, it is already a fact that this very minute you are loved by the King of kings. He is your Kinsman Redeemer. But there is also a love story for you that includes you and another. Be encouraged. Your desire is real, and it is from the

Lord. He will fulfill the desires of your heart because He is faithful.

Don't leave the Garden to venture out into the world to fulfill your heart. Stay within the Garden and abide with the One who loves you for all eternity and knows that in that Garden your Adam will come.

FOR MINE HAS, (the author Deborah says to all her readers … to be continued).

Acknowledgments

First and foremost, I want to thank my wonderful husband, Noam Cohen, for always believing in me. He has shown me that living in the Garden of Delight as husband and wife is a reality!

Next, I want to thank my five sisters – Mary Spady, Terry Sarros, Chris Maita, Vicki Felch, and Cherri Beard – for being real sisters to me and for demonstrating the authenticity of "true friendship." And a huge thank you to Terry Sarros for her help in editing this book and carrying the vision across the finish line – my deepest gratitude. To my parents, Pastor Tom and Betty Willert, thank you for naming me Deborah! And to my sons, Brian and Kevin, and their beautiful wives, Wendy and Christina, thank you for the joy you give me. And to my granddaughter, Aubrey, my little princess.

Only through the direction and inspiration of the Lord can any vision be accomplished. May the marvelous God of Abraham, Isaac and Jacob, and the Messiah of Israel, Yeshua, and the wonderful Holy Spirit receive my utmost praise for being faithful to a small town girl who now resides in His Holy City, Jerusalem!

Nadiyya – Under the Olive Tree

Nadiyya had begun her day as usual, rising before the sun and making bread for her husband. Day after day she went on, not knowing if she could survive even one more in this atmosphere. Everything around her was void of life. She looked into her husband's eyes and saw an empty vessel and wondered why. She had heard the stories told around the dinner table of the land he came from. From the descriptions, she always wondered why they had left that enchanted place. Yes, she knew there had been a famine, but why abandon the land a faithful God had given to you? Why would anyone turn from a gift that came from an invisible God yet could be seen by eyes that would behold it?

She had heard her husband's family talking about the sweet wine that cascaded down from the vineyards, the smell of flowers that blanketed the hills, the abundance of grain and wheat around the large body of water up in the Northern land. She could almost hear the crushing of the olives in the olive press and taste the figs of the land. Why would you turn your back on your God and not trust His love for you?

The only gods Nadiyya had ever known were hard little idols that never spoke or loved you with the caress of their words. Their eyes only stared back at you in blankness, just like her husband's. She had never imagined that she would feel this kind of emptiness. Where was the warmth that she so wanted from her husband? Where was the life that would fill her up to overflowing?

She smelled the sweet aroma of the bread she had so lovingly

1

made with her own hands. Her mother-in-law taught her the secret of making the beautiful, crusted bread of her homeland. Chaya was a woman of strength and beauty, undiminished by the number of her years. She had the most striking hands that Nadiyya had ever seen, and she was known in the village as the woman whose hands could bring healing with a touch, comfort to the sorrowful, and loving care to those in need. Everyone wanted to come in contact with the life and kindness in her hands. Even the children of the village would run with zeal to have Chaya touch them and ruffle their hair, only to turn with the swiftness of harts and run away with glee, set free to enjoy life forever. How Nadiyya wished she had the same powerful touch in her hands; her own were so small and delicate. Yet Nadiyya knew that her Creator, who, although unseen, was the One who fashioned her into the woman she was.

Nadiyya's hands enclosed her small waist as she slipped them down over her slight yet womanly body. She remembered that at the time of their consecration, her husband took pleasure in her body, but since he grew cold and sickly, that had changed. Once, he found her body to be his home, where she knew he felt safe and secure as he laid his head between her breasts during the night hours. Those days were gone. Now she shivered as she felt the coldness from his darting glances, as though he wished her to be sick instead of him.

The daylight hours lingered forever. And at night, her husband's weak body prevented him from reaching out to her. But more than that, she realized that his manhood had stopped desiring her. It had become clear that he did not want her to feel love during his bitter days, nor, she believed, to feel love and find love after he was gone. How lonely she felt as each day passed. Nadiyya longed for a hiding place where she could rest and be at peace within, where the sorrow and unhappiness of life could not reach her.

Nadiyya had not laughed in the last few years of her life and she had resigned herself to the fact that laughter and joy would probably not come again in her lifetime. She and Salma, her sister-in-law, at least shared that much in common; Salma had no sense of happiness in her life, either. Nadiyya had felt that if only they could form a friendship, even a friendship bound in sorrow could bring some comfort. But it was not to be. Salma's jealousy did not allow her to look into Nadiyya's heart to see a real friend; it only allowed her to see a rival. And the love she witnessed between Nadiyya and their mother-in-law increased her resentment all the more. So much pain in both hearts, and with each passing day, the mountains inside grew bigger, pushing their way to the surface and becoming visible to the outside world.

Nadiyya decided that she would make the most of the pain she lived in and would find the beauty of life in the beautiful things of nature. She found a favorite place of escape in the nearby olive grove. It had become a refuge for her heart to be able to run and frolic like a little girl. She knew it was so silly and unrestrained of her to feel so free, but something about the olive tree gave her strength as it steadfastly continued to produce all that the people of the earth needed to live. She marveled at what even one tree could produce and the variety of gifts the olive tree gave to its owner. It was virtually impossible to kill an olive tree, and even when it looked like it was dead, a shoot would spring forth and life would enter back into its branches.

Nadiyya enjoyed the beauty of the landscape around her, taking it in as though it could somehow penetrate her cold and lonely inside world. Not even Nadiyya's mother in law, Chaya, with all her words of encouragement, could erase the sadness of her marriage. And Chaya knew that if she could not bring the inward joy of life to Nadiyya, then Salma was, without a doubt, unreachable. Both husbands were so cold and unfeeling, and their hearts grew harder as they forgot the God they had left for a foreign land.

There is not one woman on this earth who does not desire the love of a man towards her – not for what he can her give in practical things, but for his passionate love of her heart. Over time, Nadiyya admitted this to be true because her own heart had finally crossed over in honesty, which did bring a freedom to her, but still the freedom was void of the true love her heart craved.

She did know that her mother-in-law's love toward her was limitless and she was grateful for that, for it gave her strength to continue on. But her sister-in-law's jealousy grew because of her own misery. Salma resented her because her own body was too round and too full for her young frame, while Nadiyya's was lovely – slight yet curvy in all the right places. Nadiyya's hair was thick and beautiful, a spiraling braid that flowed like molasses down her perfect back. Salma's hair was very thin with not a curl in sight.

Even so, Nadiyya loved her and would try to help, but as many times as Nadiyya suggested certain hennas for Salma's hair, the worse Salma's attitude became towards her. Nadiyya, of course, would always compliment her on her beautiful brown eyes and her long eyelashes, but not even these beautiful attributes could hide the bitterness of her heart. Salma came from an elite family of high standing, and her father had thought that an alliance with the foreigners could increase his export business quite handsomely. But the increase never came. Before their business arrangement could even get off the ground, Chaya's husband became ill. He had fled his homeland because of the fear of famine there. But news had traveled across the water to them that their God, who had always provided milk and honey for His people, was faithful, and the land once again flowed with abundance, as usual, for all His people to enjoy.

But it was too late for Salma's father-in-law, as Chaya and the men of the village laid his body in a cave. And soon after, Salma's own husband died of a mysterious affliction that caused his body to break out in huge boils. And not long after that, Nadiyya's own husband grew weaker and weaker and death rode in once again and took him, too. How sad the outcome of life sometimes is, even when there is so much to live for. A heavy shroud had come and lay upon their dwelling. Nadiyya struggled just to catch her breath. What would become of her and the women of her family now?

One day, Chaya marched in and simply announced to her daughters-in-law, "I am going home!" Nadiyya had dreamed about the land with the One God who had taken her husband's family out of Egypt long ago, rescuing them from Pharaoh. It made sense for Chaya to return there to her family, but what about her? What could she do? The answer was in her heart. She would follow Chaya to the land of the God who loved His people. But before she could speak it out, Chaya looked at Nadiyya and said, "I am leaving, and you must stay here with your people." Nadiyya's heart began to sink. "No, I have no one here who would care if I lived or died. You are my family now, and I have a desire to know this 'One God.' Please, Chaya, do not leave me here. I beg you." The words flooded out of the chambers of her aching heart. They were like hidden treasures that were now being revealed to the hearing ears that would hopefully listen to her longing to be loved.

Nadiyya would never forget the look in Chaya's eyes. Streams of light came cascading down upon her mother-in-law's countenance. In that moment, Nadiyya knew that Chaya saw the earnestness in her heart and that she would not leave her in this barren land of many gods. She felt Chaya's hand touch hers, and with that touch came the knowledge that life had begun for her. Chaya did not know what was waiting for them on the "unknown" side of the veil. So much time had passed since her husband took them away from that enchanted land. But her mind was made up to find out. A determination had entered her aged body, a body waiting to be filled with the sweet wine of her homeland. A body longing to rest and be comforted in the shade of a beautiful olive tree. This was her heart's desire.

There was so much to do, as all three women prepared to cross over to their husbands' birthplace. As they were about to start their journey, Salma abruptly changed her mind and decided to stay put in her misery. She did not have the vision to see beyond the veil to a new life. Nadiyya's heart ached for her sister-in-law, even though she had never felt any tenderness from her. And even though they shared a common background, deep inside they were different. Salma had always kept the pagan ways of their people. Every day, she had knelt to pay homage to idols of stone. Nadiyya would see her walk to the local temple full of idols, where people cried out in desperation to the empty stones. Salma, like Nadiyya, was childless, and wanted her womb to be filled with life. The fertility idols that Salma and her husband had kept in their chamber were detestable to Nadiyya's spirit. So distorted these frozen idols were with their forms twisted together in cold, motionless positions in a disgusting display. The priest of the temple would convince heart-broken couples that if they gave their prayers to the perverted idols, a child would be produced in their frenzy of coming together.

Nadiyya witnessed no evidence of love coming from the priests of the gods of this land to its people, and she always felt the people were being manipulated by them. The thought of the degrading rituals that were forced upon the people made Nadiyya sick to her stomach, but she was thankful that even her cold and uncaring husband had never once brought a fertility god into their chamber. The words he had heard all his life from his precious mother, Chaya, must have somehow penetrated his cold heart and reminded him that their God was holy and pure. But obviously, Salma and her husband did not heed those words.

The two women said their good byes to Salma, fearing for her life as they left, and turned toward the land of Chaya's ancestors. Something inside told Nadiyya she was coming home to her way of life, too, and that she would finally have the family she had desired for so long. She believed that one day she would look around a table and see the family that she belonged to and that belonged to her. She believed that she was going to fit into the family of Chaya's ancestors, even though she would be crossing over as a foreigner into their way of life and their God.

Her heart began to pound with excitement, and every part of her body began to tingle and shiver at the same time. Nadiyya knew that she would even have the same passion for the trees of the land of Israel that she had seen in her mother-in-law. And the olive tree, in whose shade she would sit and feel safe, would welcome her as a foreigner, taking her into its fullness. She somehow felt that she belonged to the wild branches that she had seen grow amongst the natural branches of the olive tree. And she, too, would produce fruit for her mother-in-law's people and their land. She would not take from them, but would be cultivated into the richness of these people, who would now be her people.

Her body began to tremble with such intensity that she could not contain it. It began first in her heart and then spread throughout her entire being. Would their God welcome her? Where would they live? How would they survive? Would she ever have love in this land with a man who would welcome her into his heritage? Did such a man exist? And if so, would she ever meet such a man? Those answers would come in time. Right now, all she knew for sure was that at the very moment she crossed over from her land into the unknown, she would run to the first olive tree she saw and embrace its fullness in her heart.

The start of the new day sparked a fire that Nadiyya had never felt before in her inward parts. It was as if her body was about to be consumed by a passion that it had never known. Chaya greeted her with a smile that seemed to be touched by the kiss of the unknown God that Nadiyya was about to meet. She knew, though, that it would be by faith that she would know Him, and not by touch. She was still convinced in her heart that it was the God of Israel who was the true God and who had silently and invisibly watched over her and was waiting for her to come home to His place of abundance. She was ready!

It was a long day's journey as they crossed over and entered the land of promise, and her heart began to soar like the birds that flew with grace above her head. She, too, was soaring in beauty and splendor as she closed her eyes and imagined that someone would take her as his own and love her. As she began to ponder the God of Israel who loved His people and gave them this land to cultivate and to multiply into a beautiful family, she knew that she had somehow become a part of the eternal plan of the invisible God.

She opened her eyes and the first thing they beheld was a beautiful olive tree whose leaves glistened as they twirled in the springtime breeze. Its strong trunk was gnarled by years of determination that it would live and not die. Its fruit gave forth oil that turned night into day as it burned in the lamps, creating mysterious shadows against the walls of dwelling places. She remembered Chaya's words about Solomon's temple and the purest oil filling the menorah that stood in the secret place where the priest ministered to God.

The medicine that flowed from the rich olive could touch the pain of a body that needed comfort. And its soft oil would spread over a woman's body, sealing it from the harshness of the sun and leaving a glow that welcomed the touch of a husband's hand upon his wife's willingness to give herself to him and become one. It provided fine oil for the daily meals, which also brought cleansing to the inside of the body, keeping it free from that which would clutter up its temple courts. It washed away debris and left a smooth path for good things to come inside.

Oh, how she welled up with pride at the thought of becoming part of this ancient tree that seemed to tell her a story of survival. Like the enduring olive tree before her, she would also endure to give herself to the God of Israel and to the husband who would take his tallit and cover her body with his love and devotion.

She looked at Chaya for approval to run ahead, and of course, Chaya's response came through her eyes, filled with emotion. "Run, my precious daughter. Run with the swiftness of a gazelle and embrace that which has been waiting for you." Nadiyya ran without touching the ground and molded herself into the olive tree. It couldn't have been a more perfect fit. She knew she belonged, and she lingered there, drinking in the fullness of the realization.

At that very sacred moment, she looked up and saw the most magnificent Man riding an elegant white horse that carried Him as though it were carrying royalty to His destiny of desire. Nadiyya met His countenance with her deep blue eyes, and in the warmth of that gaze, their hearts were forever melted together. Life had given her a new beginning to learn, love and desire her true place for this season in her life. As she beheld Him, the Man on the horse lifted up a natural branch and bent down to her and said, "Welcome home."

Thoughts to Meditate on:

In the book of Ruth is a picture of the church in this hour. There are two daughters-in-law in this picture. One is Ruth and the other is Orpah. Listen to the words of Naomi as she spoke from her heart. "But Naomi said, 'Turn back, my daughters; why will you go with me? Are there still sons in my womb, that they may be your husbands? Turn back, my daughters, go – for I am too old to have a husband. If I should say I have hope, if I should have a husband tonight and should also bear sons, would you wait for them till they were grown? Would you restrain yourselves from having husbands? No, my daughters; for it grieves me very much for your sakes that the hand of the LORD has gone out against me!' Then they lifted up their voices and wept again; and Orpah kissed her mother-in-law, but Ruth clung to her. And she said, 'Look, your sister-in-law has gone back to her people and to her gods; return after your sister-in-law.' But Ruth said: 'Entreat me not to leave you, Or to turn back from following after you; For wherever you go, I will go; And wherever you lodge, I will lodge; Your people shall be my people, And your God, my God. Where you die, I will die, And there will I be buried. The LORD do so to me, and more also, If anything but death parts you and me.' When she saw that she was determined to go with her, she stopped speaking to her." Ruth 1:11-18 (NKJV)

What will you do in this hour as a daughter of the King? Will you love His people unconditionally? Will you die for them? Will you have a determination in this hour to stand when others forsake you? One daughter-in-law left and went back to her foreign gods, but Ruth followed her heart into the land that she knew would give her life and to the one God who she knew would give her a relationship.

In my own life, I never knew where I belonged. Who was this Jesus that I now know as Yeshua? To me, Jesus was the church's Savior, not Israel's. I did not know, nor was I ever taught to love His people. When I fell in love with Yeshua, I fell in love with His people. It didn't matter if they did not know how to love me back. I knew that my intimate relationship with my Messiah was because Father God brought forth my Lord out of a womb that was Jewish. He had not forgotten His covenant with His people, Israel, that He would bring forth Yeshua, God Himself, to be their Passover Lamb.

Now as a Gentile who has become a Messianic Gentile believer, I can partake of the commonwealth of Israel. I can taste the sweet wine that flows down from the mountains of Israel. I can participate, with understanding, in the seven Feasts of Israel as I celebrate in the Presence of the One who is the Feasts. His Name is Yeshua, HaMashiach. How thankful I am for the Naomis in the land who would love to take us with them, as Ruths, to the House of Bread!

Scriptures to Know in our Hearts:

Nehemiah 8:14-15 "They found written in the Law, which the LORD had commanded through Moses, that the Israelites were to live in booths during the feast of the seventh month and that they should proclaim this word and spread it throughout their towns and in Jerusalem: 'Go out into the hill country and bring back branches from olive and WILD OLIVE TREES, and from myrtles, palms and shade trees, to make booths' – as it is written." (author's comment is the two shall become ONE)

Psalm 52:8 "But I am like an olive tree flourishing in the house of God; I trust in God's unfailing love for ever and ever."

Hosea 14:5-7 "I will be like the dew to Israel; he will blossom like a lily. Like a cedar of Lebanon he will send down his roots; his young shoots will grow. His splendor will be like an olive tree, his fragrance like a cedar of Lebanon. Men will dwell again in his shade. He will flourish like the grain. He will blossom like a vine, and his fame will be like the wine from Lebanon."

Romans 11:17-24 "If some of the branches have been broken off, and you, though a wild olive shoot, have been grafted in among the others and now share in the nourishing sap from the olive root, do not boast over those branches. If you do, consider this: You do not support the root, but the root supports you. You will say then, 'Branches were broken off so that I could be grafted in.' Granted. But they were broken off because of unbelief, and you stand by faith. Do not be arrogant, but be afraid. For if God did not spare the natural branches, he will *not spare you either. Consider therefore the kindness and sternness of God: sternness to those who fell, but kindness to you, provided that you continue in his kindness. Otherwise, you also will be cut off. And if they do not persist in unbelief, they will be grafted in, for God is able to graft them in again. After all, if you were cut out of an olive tree that is wild by nature, and contrary to nature were grafted into a cultivated olive tree, how much more readily will these, the natural branches, be grafted into their OWN OLIVE TREE!"*

Prayer of Revelation:

Oh, Abba Father,

How we are full of thankfulness for Your mercy towards us as Gentiles who have come into Your light. How thankful we are for Your people, Israel, that they would welcome us as Ruths and teach us Your ways. How thankful we are that we have the Holy Bible because of Your people, Israel. Help us in this hour not to turn our backs and go back where we came from, but to follow You to Zion. Teach us to love Your people, Israel, so that we can give back to them what they have given to us, the Messiah of Israel. Let us become one in this hour and lift up holy hands and praise You in Your dwelling place.

Amen.

Galia – The Sound of The Shofar

As every handmaiden waits for the love of her life, Galia, too, waited. She longed for her knight in shining armor to come galloping across her path on His white steed and sweep her off her feet. In her dreams, images of pure bliss danced across her mind. He held Himself with such regal elegance, yet also with a lowliness that she could not explain. She always recognized Him because He held a shofar in His hand as if at any moment He would put it to His lips and sound the call of gathering for her people. But as soon as His majestic presence would ride toward her, she abruptly turned her thoughts in another direction.

She did not feel worthy. When Galia looked at the reflection of her image in the Jordan River, she did not believe her dreams would come true. The One on the white horse was too handsome, too strong, too courageous to even glance at the likes of her. Galia had felt awkward in appearance since childhood, although she could not pinpoint exactly why – she had wonderful parents who had given her a loving home and a normal childhood. But whatever the source, her thoughts were too emotional for anyone to understand, even herself, and when she tried to bring forth in words what was in her heart, her lips would scatter them in a thousand different directions. Her soul was downcast, but its longings were as real to her as the Temple Mount's longing for the Messiah to be its abiding resident forever.

This time, however, her thoughts did not turn aside. Something in this moment was different. She was compelled to look into His eyes for the first time, not even aware of what had just begun in her heart. She could not look away, and then she realized nor would He. He pulled her into the deep richness of His eyes and there she melted into the pool of love. It was His love that she began to swim in. Her body became alive from within as a divine awareness permeated her being and she somehow knew that this One was keeping her from being overtaken by loneliness. She felt a burning in her soul and saw a flame of fire leap before her eyes as she mysteriously entered into the presence of the One she loved. At last she began to live.

Suddenly, from outside her dream, Galia heard the sound of a loud shofar. Awakened from her deep sleep, she knew once more the Knight in shining armor had come to her secret midnight slumber. Now aware of many voices outside her dwelling, Galia realized that the shofar was signaling the beginning of Passover. Even as her often-repeated dream spoke of her desire to be loved and swept off her feet, she knew that her people desired the Messiah to come and rule and reign in their midst. Whenever these dreams came to her, she would awaken with such anticipation for the coming of the new day. Though her disappointment was evident when she realized it was but a dream, somehow she knew in her innermost being that the dream was real.

Slowly, Galia stretched forth her ordinary limbs, not realizing that the Creator saw her as a beautiful handmaiden of Israel. Her smooth skin, touched by the rays of the sun, reflected a warm, golden, honey color. It was exactly the same touch of golden honey the last glimmer of afternoon sun reflected upon the stones of the Temple during the Passover season. It gave her some comfort to know that she at least had that in common with the very Temple of God!

So many faces, so many people, so many languages surrounded the Temple in Jerusalem. Children with huge, excited smiles on their faces as they followed their parents through the crowds. Many little ones, caught up in the excitement, inevitably wound up clutching the robe of a mother who was not their own. Suddenly, the desperate looks told it all. Mothers quickly finding each other and exchanging tearful little faces, to everyone's relief. Galia saw it all and loved it all. Young boys, extending their steps with all their might, trying to keep up with the long, easy strides of their fathers. Wanting to feel grown up and make their fathers proud. For they knew that one day, they, too, would take their families to Jerusalem to celebrate the Feast of Passover. They, too, would take the sacrifice of a little lamb for the priest to lay before the altar as an offering to Adonai.

Galia loved watching elderly couples who walked together, with treasured memories held in their hearts. And as they waited for the Messiah to come and deliver them from the oppression of the Roman soldiers, the confident look she saw in their eyes comforted her. With bold determination, they looked to the future to see their King Messiah sitting on His throne in the Temple. The slowness of their strides did not match the eagerness of their heartbeats as they somehow tried to hasten His coming with each breath. One day nearer. One day closer. Oh, how Galia herself longed for the Messiah to come and be her King and Redeemer. Not only for her, but also for her family, Israel.

Even in the daytime, her dreams were alive. Her thoughts turned to the story she loved so much of the Moabite woman named Ruth who found her redeemer in a son of Jacob named Boaz. She wanted her life to also be a story that would give hope, even after she was gone from the earth, that all things are possible if you just trust in the dream that rests in your own bosom. She knew that Someone much greater had put that desire in her and that that One would fulfill it. Did Ruth at one time feel the same? Was she unfulfilled with her first husband who was supposed to be a man of God but who ran away from the promise of His God that said His children would never beg for bread? Did the sound of the shofar reach into Ruth's pagan homeland to penetrate the ears of a handmaiden who cried out to know the true God? How Ruth must have felt when she looked at her husband and wondered why he was not hearing the shofar of his people to return home, but yet in her heart she believed she heard it.

As Galia heard the sound of the shofar blowing triumphantly over the land to summon the people to begin the Feast of Passover, her heart responded with happiness. She also rejoiced that the sound of the shofar at the onset of the Sabbath commanded her people to set aside their normal work and to rest in the Presence of their God. He worked for six days creating what she saw every day, the beauty of the world around her and the beauty of man walking in it, enjoying God's creation for them.

Her Uncle Elimelech would frequently remind her that it was the sound of the shofar that summoned Moses to receive the Torah on Mount Sinai. Her family would wait with such anticipation for the beginning of the New Year, Rosh HaShanah, when the shofar would pierce the heavens in celebration that the God of Israel had given His people, Israel, another new year to be able to live in His Ways. She loved this day, especially, because the shofar was blown one hundred times. It was a thundering force that vibrated against every Jewish heart to be awakened to His power over all the enemies of Israel. It was a reminder to her people of their own words as they stood at the base of Mt. Sinai and responded to Moses with, "Na'aseh V'nishma". Those words of commitment resonated in her own heart, together with those who had voiced it ages ago, "We will obey and then understand." Her uncle would explain that the shofar is a holy instrument, blown by skillful men of God.

She reprimanded herself for allowing her thoughts to run away again, making her absentmindedly wander for a time, forgetting her tasks. Galia was in a hurry to purchase the sweet wine for her family's Passover seder. Her father always knew exactly when Jacob the winemaker would make his way into Jerusalem and would send her to get the precious fruit of the vine. Jacob had a gift with the beautiful grapes that had been prized by their ancestors for centuries. Galia was sure that just as Caleb and Joshua were exhilarated to hold the cluster of grapes bursting with juice, Jacob swelled with the same pride as he handled this treasure that God had promised to Israel long ago and that her people now enjoyed.

Suddenly, a holy scripture came to mind and she recited it in her thoughts, "I will lift up the cup of salvation and call on the name of the LORD." Oh, how rich her people were with the abundance of provision from their God. He provided for Abraham, Isaac, Jacob and their children and their children's children, right down to this very moment in her own life. She wanted, from the very core of her heart, to hold and touch the One who the prophets said would deliver Israel from oppression and fear, the Messiah who was promised to come and save her people. She believed that just as God had delivered them from Pharaoh, He would deliver them from the Roman fist.

Smelling the air of excitement, feeling the cobblestones worn smooth by thousands of sandals, Galia made her way to the special place where Jacob always sold the precious wine treasure to his long-time customers. In the bustle, she stumbled into a man carrying a huge water vessel and almost knocked him down. How could she be so careless, not paying more attention? Afraid that she had upset the man, Galia profusely apologized and asked his forgiveness, but he seemed unconcerned. His water vessel was intact, and he had managed to juggle it without one drop of water spilling to the dusty stones beneath his feet. He told her that he was fine, but that he was in a hurry to take the vessel to a room he was preparing for the Messiah.

What?! She could not believe her ears. "Messiah"? Surely, she must have misunderstood his word. Surely he must have just said "Master." But again, he said "The Messiah's room is being prepared for the Passover seder meal." He turned and left. Galia stood still in total disbelief and even touched her ears to make sure they weren't somehow absent. No, everything was in place, and she could hear the turtledoves cooing to each other. But her heart was beating wildly, and her legs were not finding the strength to take even a step. "The Messiah"? She longed to see Him, touch Him, smell the fragrance of the One who came to her in her dreams.

Galia collected herself, and remembering her task, she set off to ascend to the winemaker, Jacob. But on the way, an unseen force caused her to stop in her tracks, knowing she must find the man with the water vessel. She spun around and ran back to where they had collided. Looking to see where he might have gone, she noticed movement in an outer courtyard, and to her amazement, saw the man. He was speaking intently to Someone who filled the entire atmosphere with His presence. Hardly moving, yet drawn in, she breathed this atmosphere into the depths of her being.

What was happening to her? She felt intoxicated, but had not had a drop of sweet wine. Everything in her came alive. She looked down at her trembling hands and as she raised her eyes, He turned and looked at her. She finally beheld the One who held the shofar in her dreams. The flame of her heart began to dance!

Thoughts To Meditate On:

We as non-Jews (Goyim) have so much to learn from Yeshua's family. Most of what has been passed down to us by the church has been taken as truth without our being good Bereans of the Word of God. Every one of us wants to respect and honor those who are in leadership over us, but many times we take instructions that are not the instructions from the Word.

Let's take a look at the shofar, for instance. What is it? What does it have to do with the modern 21st century Christian? Why would we bring an ancient instrument into a modern setting with stained glass windows and padded pews? Why is the shofar important to us who are grafted into the Olive tree? What sounds from this instrument, if any, are we to know? And are we to respond to the different sounds the shofar gives forth?

As I look back at my own walk on the Ancient Path with the Ruach HaKodesh (Holy Spirit), I realize why He took me directly to the shofar in the land and the revelation of the shofar, which, of course, is Israel. He began to teach me how important it was for our new fellowship, birthed by the Spirit of God, to bring forth the sound of the shofar and to understand its significance – that the Holy Spirit would begin to penetrate our hearing and bring forth knowledge, which would lead to action as we responded to the sound that commands attention and points with honor and respect toward King Yeshua. The atmosphere of our fellowship began to change. Some people responded with the utmost contempt and, of course, walked out of the sanctuary, while simultaneously, other people's hearts melted with tears and the words, "How come I never knew about this instrument of the Lord?" The shofar always blows the chaff away from the threshing floor of His house.

We now know from the story of Galia how the shofar announced the coming of the Sabbath and holidays to the Jewish people. At the coronation of kings, you would hear the shofar blowing with the announcement, "THE KING IS IN RESIDENCE." It was also used to summon the troops of Israel to gather for a battle against the enemies who would rise against them. We all know the stories of Gideon's victory at the camp of Midian and Joshua's victory at Jericho, and the role that the ram's horn (shofar) played in each of them. The story of Galia reminds us of how the shofar blew on Mt. Sinai to bring Moses to attention to receive the commandments that God had set forth for His people to walk in.

When I stand under the majestic sound of the shofar coming forth as it sweeps over a congregation, everything in me comes alive. It is a reminder of the faithfulness of the God of Abraham, Isaac and Jacob and that He is coming back to receive His bride with such celebration. Even the patterns of the long and short blasts of the shofar speak different instructions to the ears of the hearer. They are God's special sound-codes to the inhabitants of His kingdom.

As we come to this final curtain call on God's stage for all the world to see, we the believers, will hear the final ram's horn being blown to lift us up into the arms of our beloved Redeemer and Bridegroom, Yeshua. These are thoughts to meditate on in the night hours when your soul is quiet, to be instructed by the Wind of the Spirit as He brings forth truth of His eternal Word.

Scriptures To Know And Store In Our Hearts:

Genesis 22:13-14 "Abraham looked up and there in a thicket he saw a ram caught by its horns. He went over and took the ram and sacrificed it as a burnt offering instead of his son. So Abraham called that place The LORD Will Provide. And to this day it is said, 'On the mountain of the LORD it will be provided.'"

Exodus 19:13 "'He shall surely be stoned or shot with arrows; not a hand is to be laid on him. Whether man or animal, he shall not be permitted to live.' Only when the ram's horn sounds a long blast may they go up to the mountain."

Numbers 10:9 "When you go into battle in your own land against an enemy who is oppressing you, sound a blast on the trumpets. Then you will be remembered by the LORD your God and rescued from your enemies."

Joshua 6:4-5 "Have seven priests carry trumpets of rams' horns in front of the ark. On the seventh day, march around the city seven times, with the priests blowing the trumpets. When you hear them sound a long blast on the trumpets, have all the people give a loud shout; then the wall of the city will collapse and the people will go up, every man straight in."

Judges 6:34 "Then the Spirit of the Lord came upon Gideon, and he blew a trumpet, summoning the Abiezrites to follow him."

Judges 7:18 "When I and all who are with me blow our trumpets, then from all around the camp blow yours and shout, 'For the LORD and for Gideon.'"

1 Samuel 13:3 "Jonathan attacked the Philistine outpost at Geba, and the Philistines heard about it. Then Saul had the trumpet blown throughout the land and said, 'Let the Hebrews hear!'"

2 Samuel 6:15 "... while he and the entire house of Israel brought up the ark of the LORD with shouts and the sound of trumpets."

1 King 1:34 "There have Zadok the priest and Nathan the prophet anoint him king over Israel. Blow the trumpet and shout, 'Long live King Solomon!'"

Matthew 24:31 "And he will send his angels with a loud trumpet call, and they will gather his elect from the four winds, from one end of the heavens to the other."

1 Corinthians 15:52 "... in a flash, in the twinkling of an eye, at the last trumpet. For the trumpet will sound, the dead will be raised imperishable, and we will be changed."

1 Thessalonians 4:16 "For the Lord himself will come down from heaven, with a loud command, with the voice of the archangel and with the trumpet call of God, and the dead in Christ will rise first."

Prayer of Revelation

Dear Abba Father,

How we welcome the sound of the shofar to resound in our own temples to awaken us to Your coming. Pierce our ears with Your sword and let the sound of the shofar bring freedom to our walk with You. May we receive this holy instrument into our lives to rehearse the sound of Your coming. May it remind us to come to attention and separate ourselves in this hour for Your holiness to be seen in us. And may it be a constant reminder of the faithfulness of Your coming.

B'shem Yeshua,

Amen.

Leah – The Wooden Mezuzzah

Leah awoke to a cold, windy, wet day in Bet Shemesh. For her people, Israel, the rain was a blessing, and, despite the chill in her bones, she was trying to remain thankful for this blessing. She opened the door of her small dwelling and already felt the weather challenge her errands for the day. The small bushes around her door were bending low at the assault of the wind coming down the corridor to her abode. It became obvious as she stepped into the street that no one else had ventured out for the day.

Leah had always been one whose eyes popped open with the first song of the birds that perched upon the fig tree outside the room where she laid her head at night. Sometimes she would awake before they did and would rouse them with her own song of thanksgiving to Adonai. The words would flow out of her like a gentle stream at first, and as she gathered her breath, they would burst forth like the rushing waters of the Jordan that flowed through the Hula Valley at flood stage.

Today, her song of thanksgiving reminded her of her childhood when her Uncle Mordecai would take her on outings to the Jordan River. His hand, calloused by many hours of tightly holding the scribe's writing instrument, would also tightly hold her little fingers, forgetting how small and delicate they were. He was not aware of the strength that had formed in the muscles of his hand as it held the kosher quill pen day after day. Even though he was a strong man in the natural, Leah knew that much of the strength coming through his hand was divine strength that came from writing the

21

Ancient Words of Torah. With precision, he would inscribe the words of the Shema on parchments which were then enclosed within beautifully carved wooden mezuzzahs and attached to the doorposts of every Jewish dwelling.

People in her village gave her uncle their respect because of his calling as a scribe to copy the Words of Instruction that had been given to Moses by the voice of Yahweh. They respected the calling on his life, but Leah knew that most of them secretly thanked Adonai for their own status as farmers, bakers and tailors - men of labor - rather than being the one to sit for hours by candlelight over the parchment. Uncle Mordecai would always say to her that before the world was created, Yahweh had already determined who would hold the kosher quill pen and who would hold the reins of the oxen.

Leah always enjoyed going to the market to buy a new writing instrument for her Uncle Mordecai. There were three shops to choose from, but she had her favorite. It was the shop of the family of her best friend, Maya. It would be more expensive there, but the quality would be of excellence. Maya's father went to the most respectable farmer in the area to select the kosher fowl that would produce the perfect feather writing quill. Leah loved to hear Maya talk of her family's journeys to purchase these flawless fowls. They would set out early in the morning to travel to Beersheba where they were sold. She would describe in detail the little villages that they passed through, most of which did not even have names, but where families had gathered to build their homes near a well that had been re-dug. Extended families would come from all over the region just to be together. They would set up a community surrounding the house of the Rabbi. As long as there was a Rabbi in the village, they were settled in their hearts that the blessing of HaShem would be upon them.

On one such trip, Maya's family had passed a caravan of very important-looking tribesmen from a distant land, unlike the spice caravans from Egypt that they had seen before. Some of these men looked like kings, arrayed in splendorous embroidered robes, and the countless camels were laden with precious cargo. Someone had heard that they were astrologers or very wise men. Her family wondered where this prestigious group could possibly be going and who they could possibly be going to see. Typical questions of her people. Everyone in Israel was known to be extremely inquisitive about everything and everyone, from their closest neighbor to any stranger traveling through their land. Others said their curiosity was just too much and that they should mind their own business. But she could not agree. Maya believed that her people truly loved everybody and wanted to reach out to anyone who might need assistance. Her people were always gracious to the foreigner who came through their Promised Land.

Oh, how Leah longed for a life of adventure like that of her friend Maya! Maya got to leave her village many times to go on these journeys, but Leah had only journeyed from one side of Jerusalem to the other. Leah was thankful, though, because she was privileged to live in the most beautiful city in all the region, with the great temple rising from the center of Mt. Moriah. She had only to look outside her doorway to see the mountains surrounding Jerusalem and the glow of the sun dancing upon the stones leading up to the steps of Herod's temple. Even though her friend Maya would visit Beersheba every new moon and see the beauty of the desert, Leah would be content with her own journeys in the holy city of Yahweh. But even so, maybe today Leah would hear another exciting story about a caravan of kings bringing gifts to someone in Jerusalem or maybe in the small village of Bethlehem.

As she neared the shop, Leah turned her thoughts back to the important task at hand, selecting the best possible writing instrument for her uncle. She understood the seriousness of attaching the mezuzzah to the lintels of their homes. There was a holy awe that settled upon her as she kissed her delicate fingers, touched the carved mezuzzah, and then brought her fingers back to her pink lips. Her Uncle Mordecai had told her of the kindness of Yahweh to allow His Word to be put upon their small dwellings. There were times that Leah would run her fingers across the letter

Shin and feel goose bumps rise and fall on her olive-colored arms. It was as though she could feel the kiss of the Ancient of Days being placed upon her each time she touched the beautiful object that held His Word within it.

Before entering the shop, Leah touched the mezuzzah and, of course, the goose bumps came. And along with them came a warmth and anticipation in her whole being. She was overcome with thankfulness for Jerusalem and for the people who lived in this Holy City. They were real people with a real commitment to the Holy Script. Everything in Leah's life centered around the Shekinah glory that her people longed for. Her people were waiting for the Messiah to come and to sit in the Holy temple as King over Israel.

Leah's desire was the same. But within that desire was another desire – a secret one she had not shared with anyone – not her Uncle Mordecai – not even Maya. Her deepest desire was that she herself could become a "living" mezuzzah, a vessel carved by God Himself, with His Word written upon her very own heart.

Was it possible that one day this desire would come to pass, or had her imagination taken over? Until she knew for sure, Leah would continue to kiss and touch the Shema within the carved wooden mezuzzah. She clasped her hands to her chest, vowing to keep her desire a secret until the Messiah of her people, Israel, would Himself come and inscribe His Word upon the parchment of her heart. With fresh hope, Leah looked up and beheld a caravan of royalty passing by at that very moment. Who were they coming to see?

Thoughts to Meditate On:

As Christians who have accepted the blood of the Jewish Messiah Jesus to wash away our sins and to save us from the bowels of hell, we need to understand all the symbols that the Lord has shown His people to remember Him in their lives. Now that we have bound ourselves to His instructions, we can begin to understand the Lord's mercy to us by allowing us to have these same symbols in our own walk with Him.

You will soon see that instead of being separate from each other, the Jew and the Gentile will become one as we incorporate the symbols of Israel into our lives. One such symbol is the mezuzzah that the Jewish people attach to their doorposts as a reminder of His Word in their daily lives.

The Hebrew letter "Shin", which is always placed upon the mezuzzah, is the abbreviation of one of God's names, Shaddai. One of the many mezuzzahs that I have purchased as gifts, had three Hebrew letters on it - Shin, Dalet and Yod. It spells out the words "The Guardian of the Gates of Israel." When you travel to Israel, you will find that numerous artists have their own unique mezuzzah designs to showcase their talents. The variety of the mezuzzah is endless, with colors and shapes of every description.

The scriptures that are placed in the mezuzzah are from the book of Deuteronomy. The first and foremost scripture is Deuteronomy 6:4-9; "Hear, O Israel: The LORD our God, the LORD is one! You shall love the LORD your God with all your heart, with all your soul, and with all your strength.

"And these words which I command you today shall be in your heart. You shall teach them diligently to your children, and shall talk of them when you sit in your house, when you walk by the way, when you lie down, and when you rise up. You shall bind them as a sign on your hand and they shall be as frontlets between your eyes. You shall write them on the doorposts of your house and on your gates." NKJV

The other scripture that is written on this delicate parchment is Deuteronomy 11:13-21; "And it shall be that if you earnestly obey My commandments which I command you today, to love the LORD your God and serve Him with all your heart and with all your soul, then I will give you the rain for your land in its season, the early rain and the latter rain, that you may gather in your grain, your new wine, and your oil. And I will send grass in your fields for your livestock, that you may eat and be filled. Take heed to yourselves, lest your heart be deceived, and you turn aside and serve other gods and worship them, lest the LORD's anger be aroused against you, and He shut up the heavens so that there be no rain, and the land yield no produce, and you perish quickly from the good land which the LORD is giving you.

Therefore you shall lay up these words of mine in your heart and in your soul, and bind them as a sign on your hand, and they shall be as frontlets between your eyes. You shall teach them to your children, speaking of them when you sit in your house, when you walk by the way, when you lie down, and when you rise up. And you shall write them on the doorposts of your house and on your gates, that your days and the days of your children may be multiplied in the land of which the LORD swore to your fathers to give them, like days of the heavens above the earth." NKJV

Now let's take these scriptures into the "Renewed Testament" and see what the Lord instructs us to do about the writings on the parchment called the mezuzzah. 1 Corinthians 15:46 says, "The spiritual did not come first, but the natural, and after that the spiritual." Everything that the Israelites were told to do in the natural has become such a blessing for those of us who did not grow up with an understanding of the Jewish ways of life. Because Yeshua is Jewish and we are preparing ourselves to be His bride, we take on His ways of life, not ours, just as an earthly wife who leaves her ways behind and chooses to live for her husband. When you fall in love with someone, you want to please him. As believers in Yeshua, we are so blessed to learn of our Jewish brothers and sisters, and we now have the responsibility to look at the Renewed testament through Jewish eyes. We must always remember that it is a Jewish book and not a Gentile book.

2 Corinthians 3:3 "You show that you are a letter from Christ (Messiah), the result of our ministry, written not with ink but with the Spirit of the living God, not on tablets of stone, but on tablets of human hearts." Even though we are not Jewish, our Lord is. The Lord has given us so many things to remind of us His love and provision every day. One of these reminders is the mezuzzah that we can attach to the doorways of our homes.

As we come and go from our dwelling places, we can be reminded that we have His Word written in our hearts. We become a letter of His goodness read by all we meet on our life's journey. Hebrews 10:16; "This is the covenant I will make with them after that time, says the Lord. I will put my laws in their hearts, and I will write them on their *minds." We know that this scripture is spoken to His people Israel, but now, as the wild olive branches, we can receive the promise with them as brothers and sisters together in the Messiah's Name.*

Scriptures To Know And Store In Our Hearts:

<u>2 Corinthians 3:3</u> *"You show that you are a letter from Christ (Messiah), the result of our ministry, written not with ink but with the Spirit of the living God, not on tablets of stone, but on tablets of human hearts."*

<u>Proverbs 7:2-3</u> *"Keep my commands and you will live; guard my teachings as the apple of your eye. Bind them on your fingers; write them on the tablet of your heart."*

<u>Proverbs 3:1-2</u> *" My son, do not forget my teaching, but keep my commands in your heart, for they will prolong your life many years and bring you prosperity."*

<u>Psalm 40:8</u> *" I desire to do your will, O my God; your law is within my heart."*

<u>Psalm 37:30-31</u> *" The mouth of the righteous man utters wisdom, and his tongue speaks what is just. The law of his God is in his heart; his feet do not slip."*

<u>Romans 10:8-13</u> *" But what does it say? 'The word is near you; it is in your mouth and in your heart,' that is, the word of faith we are proclaiming: That if you confess with your mouth, 'Jesus is Lord,' and believe in your heart that God raised him from the dead, you will be saved. For it is with your heart that you believe and are justified, and it is with your mouth that you confess and are saved. As the Scripture says, 'Anyone who trusts in him will never be put to shame.' For there is no difference between Jew and Gentile -- the same Lord is Lord of all and richly blesses all who call on him, for, 'Everyone who calls on the name of the Lord will be saved.'"*

Prayer of Revelation:

Abba, Father,

How thankful we are that Your people Israel kept Your ways and held them dear to their hearts. That generation after generation, they have upheld Your ways for the nations to see. Reveal to us as Messianic Gentiles how to cling to Your ways. Teach us how to receive insight where we were blind before. Open our eyes to see that You have extended grace to us in our ignorance of Your symbols before us. Forgive us for our pride, that we thought we were the ones to show our Jewish brothers and sisters how to live, but in reality, they are here to show us how to live before the Lord each day. We thank You and praise You that their gifts and their call are irrevocable. We now receive Your ways through Your people with a fresh understanding.

In the name of Yeshua,

Amen.

Talli – The Sabbath Candles

She wanted so badly to perform all the mitzvot that came her way, but she was feeling the weariness in her bones. Talli's life had become so busy - going to the marketplace weekly to buy the flour she needed to make her sweet-smelling bread, purchasing her fresh cinnamon and other herbs at the spice shop on the other side of Jerusalem every Yom Rishon, visiting her grandmother in the next village every Yom Shi Shi to attend to her needs, babysitting her neighbor's children twice a week so her neighbor could earn a few extra shekels to make ends meet after losing her husband in a terrible fall. Besides doing all of the normal things her own life required, she could never say no to anyone who needed her help, knowing it was the right thing to do, even if it meant that she would have to get up earlier and go to bed later than anyone else she knew.

It had always been that way in her life. She could still hear her elderly grandfather's voice as he used to sit and read the ancient scrolls to her. "Talli, calm yourself in the Almighty. He knows your very thoughts and will comfort you like He did Sarah." Talli waited patiently for that day to come, but life went on as usual. It is not to say that she felt unthankful for her life, because that was not it at all. She had all she needed. Her cupboards were full of food, she had shelter, and she was covered with beautiful garments that she skillfully fashioned. Still, she was tired. She figured there must be something wrong with her, and that she must find the ability to face her trials just as her own ancestors had faced their trials before

29

her.

Talli loved the rich heritage of her people, Israel. She recalled the strength of Sarah, wandering in the desert with her husband, Abraham. Sarah was a princess, but found herself in a goat-haired tent surrounded by desert. She must have spent many quiet hours reflecting on the riches of her past. But Sarah had something that Talli had not yet experienced, and that was the love of a husband. One who would cultivate her garden and love her because she was, in his eyes, the most beautiful creature he had ever seen. The one that Talli would fall in love with would walk into her room and light up her life with fire. His gaze would fall upon her and consume her and draw her into his arms forever.

Trying to settle her thoughts, Talli purposed to dream only at night and not be swept away in the daylight hours. Life must go on, and no matter who was with her or who was not with her, she would live life with a smile on her face.

Today her parents came to mind, and she missed them. They both had suddenly crossed over and now rested in Abraham's bosom. She remembered the promises of the ancient scrolls that said the Ancient of Days would be her provider and He would be her portion. She struggled to believe it at the moment, though, as her body ached after a long day of chores. Wood in hand, Talli walked down the long, narrow path to her abode. Feeling the warmth of the shawl wrapped tightly around her shoulders and the chill of the cold winter night upon her cheeks, she welcomed the thought of entering her cozy, one-room dwelling. As she neared, she could see a shimmering glow coming from her little home. She had not been home to light the candles yet, so why was she seeing the glow of Sabbath candles streaming from her doorway?

Talli's heart beat rapidly. She was late in returning home for this Sabbath night, but she knew that the Almighty would be patient with her. It was never in her heart to grieve the Creator of the universe by not recognizing the sanctity of the Sabbath. She moved with trepidation toward the door. The light became brighter. Had her neighbor, Sarah, scurried in to light the Sabbath candles for Talli? No, it couldn't be. Sarah was busy with her own family's needs.

With heightened awareness of a Divine Presence coming from her dwelling, she opened the door and her own eyes confirmed it; her Sabbath candles were indeed lit. The flames swayed in the gentle wind that came through the door with Talli as if they were welcoming her home to rest. The walls were dancing with what looked like people with their hands lifted upwards toward the heavens. Talli looked with wonderment around the small, slightly furnished room, and knew in her heart that Someone had come and prepared this night for her. She felt no fear.

But why would anybody take the time to light the Sabbath candles for her to enjoy? Who would so lovingly take notice of her when there were so many other people in her village? Why single out her insignificant life to bless?

She stood so still she could hear her own heartbeat and her own breath go in and out. She had heard of angels appearing and ministering to her people, but they were all very important people in the big scheme of God's plan. She was nobody of importance. She was not from a royal family or from the priestly line of Aaron. She was from the tiny tribe of Benjamin. Oh, she knew that King Saul was from the same tribe, but he did not leave a very good impression after all. She had heard much debate about him all her life.

Talli stilled her thoughts and began to receive the peace and tranquility that was permeating her little place. It felt like her very being became part of the glow from the candles. She had no idea how long she had lingered while savoring the moment in time. This was the most wonderful Sabbath she had ever experienced. That night, as she lay upon her feather mattress, she would dream of the One who would some day say to her, "I will be the lamp in your darkness." With her hair softly cascading across the pillow, forming a crown around her lovely face, her mind was seeing images of the One who had come to her dwelling. Yes, there was Someone who had come and lit the candles in her little one-room dwelling. But who was it?

Talli believed with all of her heart that one day very soon, she would meet that One who would, in every way, light up her darkness.

Thoughts To Meditate On:

As Christians, why have we put aside the lighting of the candles which honors the Lord of the Sabbath? What do the scriptures reveal to us today, as Gentile believers, about our Jewish roots? Would the lighting of the candles enhance our relationship with Yeshua? Would we be immersed into the eternal realm and see Him, who is the Light of the World, with clearer vision?

In Isaiah 56, the Lord says that the son of the foreigner who joins himself to the Lord to serve Him and keeps the Sabbath, God will bless that one and make him joyful in God's house of prayer. Right away, the Lord gives a blessing of joy to those who keep the Sabbath. We all need in this hour the joy of the Lord, which is our strength.

The Lord also says that He will gather to Him OTHERS besides those who are gathered to Him. We know that the "others" are us who do not have Jewish blood in our veins. The beautiful picture of the lighting of the Sabbath candles, shows us that the Messiah Yeshua came forth as The Light of the World from the womb of a Jewish handmaiden. Many of my messianic friends have said that as the Jewish woman is circling the flames of the candle three times, it represents the Father, Son and Holy Spirit. Genesis 1:3 states, "And God said, 'Let there be light', and there was light." We, as believers in the Light of the World, can be so enhanced in revelation when we begin to honor the Sabbath with the lighting of the Sabbath candles.

When Moses was facing off with Pharaoh, there is a scripture that so vividly describes the difference between the kingdom of darkness and the Kingdom of light. Exodus 10:21-23; "Then the LORD said to Moses, 'Stretch out your hand toward the sky so that darkness will spread over Egypt—darkness that can be felt.' So Moses stretched out his hand toward the sky, and total darkness covered all Egypt for three days. No one could see anyone else or leave his place for three days. Yet all the Israelites had LIGHT in the places where they lived.'" This is such a beautiful picture of the Sabbath evening. There is darkness outside, but with the Light of Yeshua in your homes there is light within. How blessed we are that our Jewish brothers and sisters have given us this tradition to remind us of who is the Light is.

When Yeshua was speaking to His family, Israel, at the Mt. of Beatitudes, he spoke this exhortation in Matthew 5:15 - "Neither do people light a lamp and put it under a bowl. Instead they put it on its stand, and it gives light to everyone in the house." We have the opportunity, as those who have joined into the commonwealth of Israel, to light the Sabbath candles so that others who live in darkness can be moved to come to the Light of His Presence.

Job cried out and said, "... when his lamp shone upon my head and by his light I walked through darkness!" Job 29:3. What a promise to us that when we, in the natural, light our Sabbath candles to remember His promises to us, we are declaring to the heavenlies, "He is my Light."

Peter made a proclamation in 1 Peter 2:9-10 "But you are a chosen people, a royal priesthood, a holy nation, a people belonging to God, that you may declare the praises of him who called you out of darkness into his wonderful light. Once you were not a people, but now you are the people of God; once you had not received mercy, but now you have received mercy."

Now, as Christians who have taken on our Lord's traditions, because He is Jewish, we understand why the apostles were always pointing back to the bedrock that the prophets spoke from. "And we have the word of the prophets made more certain, and you will do well to pay attention to it, as to a light shining in a dark place, until the day dawns and the morning star rises in your hearts." 2 Peter 1:19.

In the Temple Courts, Yeshua said to those who were listening, "I am the light of the world. Whoever follows me will never walk in darkness, but will have the light of life." John 8:12.

Scriptures To Know And Store In Our Hearts:

Isaiah 56:3-8 "Let no foreigner who has bound himself to the LORD say, 'The LORD will surely exclude me from his people.' And let not any eunuch complain, 'I am only a dry tree.' For this is what the LORD says: 'To the eunuchs who keep my Sabbaths, who choose what pleases me and hold fast to my covenant – to them I will give within my temple and its walls a memorial and a name better than sons and daughters; I will give them an everlasting name that will not be cut off. And foreigners who bind themselves to the LORD to serve him, to love the name of the LORD, and to worship him, all who keep the Sabbath without desecrating it and who hold fast to my covenant – these I will bring to my holy mountain and give them joy in my house of prayer. Their burnt offerings and sacrifices will be accepted on my altar; for my house will be called a house of prayer for all nations.' The Sovereign LORD declares – he who gathers the exiles of Israel: 'I will gather still others to them besides those already gathered.'"

Genesis 1:3 "And God said, "Let there be light, and there was light.""

Job 29:3 "... when his lamp shone upon my head and by his light I walked through darkness!"

1 Peter 2:9-10 "But you are a chosen people, a royal priesthood, a holy nation, a people belonging to God, that you may declare the praises of him who called you out of darkness into his wonderful light. Once you were not a people, but now you are the people of God; once you had not received mercy, but now you have received mercy."

2 Peter 1:19 "And we have the word of the prophets made more certain, and you will do well to pay attention to it, as to a light shining in a dark place, until the day dawns and the morning star rises in your hearts."

Isaiah 42:6-7 "I, the LORD, have called you in righteousness; I will take hold of your hand. I will keep you and will make you to be a covenant for the people and a light for the Gentiles, to open eyes that are blind, to free captives from prison and to release from the dungeon those who sit in darkness."

Prayer of Revelation:

Dear Abba, Father,

Teach us how to receive Your Words of Life to our souls. May we learn to not be afraid of the unknown traditions of Your people, Israel. May we see that all that You have commanded them to do is being revealed to us in this hour as the ones who have joined in to worship You together with Your people. The prophet Isaiah says, "I, the Lord, have called you in righteousness; I will take hold of your hand. I will keep you and will make you to be a covenant for the people and light for the Gentiles, to open eyes that are blind, to free captives from prison and to release from the dungeon those who sit in darkness."

Amen.

Hanna – The Challah Bread

Hanna rose early to begin her preparation for the Sabbath evening. Her life was good, and she could say that for the most part she was satisfied. She certainly knew that there was a richness that some others had not experienced, but still she acknowledged there was a small portion of her heart that was unfulfilled. Was she like her ancestors in that? She had often wondered why her people, Israel, spent forty years in the desert. The sages had said that her people were only three days from the land of Promise. Was she only three days from her land of Promise? As she looked down at her sandaled feet, it was obvious they were already standing in the promised land. Even so, Hanna had such an anticipation in her heart that her life was about to change. She wanted to believe that soon the Messiah would come and deliver her people from the tyranny around them.

She thought about the two spies named Y'hoshua and Kalev and was thankful for their determination to fulfill the Lord's command. These two brothers changed the course of history because of their faith in Yahweh's Word to the Israelites. They anchored their hearts to the God of Abraham, Isaac and Jacob's Word to them. Their fearlessness saved the destiny of a young generation of Israelites.

She remembered, with trembling, the words of others who defied what Adonai said to her people. "We wish we had died in the land of Egypt! Or that we had died here in the desert." They had declared to one another, "Let's go back to Egypt." She found herself overwhelmed with a thankful heart when she thought of the two faithful Israelites who stood and advanced forward into the land that Adonai gave to her people.

She remembered the manna falling from heaven for her people in the desert. "What's this?" they had asked as they looked at one another. They had become accustomed to the rich food of Egypt. The aroma of leeks and onions still lingered in their nostrils. And then Adonai let fall from the throne these thin, tiny flakes to eat. She had heard that it was like coriander seed, white, and that it tasted like honey cakes. Who was up there in heaven preparing this substance daily that sustained them? Adonai had said to Moshe, "Here, I will cause bread to rain down from heaven for you." Her people gathered twice as much on the sixth day, for Adonai told them the seventh day was a Shabbat rest for them.

Today, she was preparing her Challah bread for the Sabbath, to give as a gift to her friends Roni and Hallel. They were wonderful friends who always included her in their Sabbath festival. One thing she had noticed and loved about these friends is that there was a difference in their countenance from others she knew. They always had a beautiful glow around their faces, and they walked in a peace she did not fully understand. Often, she felt like they were on the verge of sharing a secret with her but would stop short before the words could come forth. She so desired to know the secret they held in their hearts. She longed to have their same calmness permeate her own life.

The challah that rested on her counter was so beautiful, with a golden-brown hue encasing the pure sweetness within. She could almost taste the warmth of the bread upon her tongue right now. How tempted she was to just pinch a small piece from the underside of the loaf. Surely Roni and Hallel would not notice the small tear. But, of course, she would never do that. She honored every symbol of the Sabbath table.

She carefully wrapped the special bread in the Sabbath linen napkin and tucked it in her basket. As she walked, she thought about how all of Israel would be welcoming the Sabbath tonight, knowing it would usher in the peace that her people so passionately desired in this hour. As Roni and Hallel opened the door of their home, she sensed they were also opening the doors of their hearts, and she felt as though she could literally walk right into them, feeling loved and secure. "Shabbat Shalom, Hanna. Welcome to our home. May you be embraced by the Shekinah that is His Presence." Hanna felt like she would melt in the atmosphere that welcomed her. Again, Hanna looked into the eyes of her friends and saw the light that invaded her whole being. How she wanted to have that same look in her eyes.

It was time for Hallel to welcome the Sabbath with the lighting of the candles. The right candle was lit to remember that by Adonai's hand, her people were led out of Egypt into the promised land, and the left candle was lit to observe all of Adonai's ways. Breathtakingly beautiful was Hallel as she covered her dark raven hair with her white shawl. Slowly, her deep, earth-brown, exotic eyes were hidden to block out the world from entering into the "stillness of the eternal moment." Her hands traced three elegant circles around the dancing candle flames. The ancient words filled the room with hope.

Roni then began to speak the blessing over the bread. Hanna could not help but glance into Roni's face as his mouth spoke the words. She saw strength enter into every muscle of his face. And as he raised the challah toward heaven, everything began to move in slow motion. There was a tangible Presence in the room. It seemed as though this blessing had been waiting in the atmosphere to be welcomed one more time into a Jewish home. Hanna was overwhelmed.

Why was this Sabbath so different from all the others she had experienced? Was it because she was different? Hanna felt her body begin to melt into the very essence of the sweet smelling challah bread. How she savored this moment, and how thankful she was for Roni and Hallel's obedience to the command to honor the Sabbath. Was the Presence she felt that of the Eternal God who was savoring this moment with His people, Israel, on this Sabbath eve?

Thoughts To Meditate On:

In this story of Hanna, we see the Jewish people keeping the commandment to observe and enter into the Sabbath rest. We see the continuation of faithfulness to the very words that Yahweh gave to His people. Let's look at the picture of the challah bread.

We, as Jewish and Gentile believers, need to come together in this hour as never before. We Gentile believers would never have the richness of understanding without our Jewish brothers and sisters staying exactly who they are - Jewish. They have not converted to our ways, but we have converted to their ways. At every Passover seder meal throughout the centuries to this day, we see the breaking of the matzah bread. And at each Sabbath meal, we see the breaking of the challah bread which is then sprinkled with salt to represent the covenant. At both tables, the Bread of Life is being revealed right before our eyes!

As Gentile believers, we considered Sunday our Sabbath, but the Sabbath is a day of rest with the Lord, family and friends. It is the last day of the week, where we are to rest and give thanks to the Lord for sustaining for the first six days. We have missed the day of enjoyment and resting and not doing any work. How we have fallen off of the ancient path and have gone further and further away from the bedrock of the foundation of the Written Word.

In the holy of holies was the table of shewbread, which translates as "The table of His face." Every Sunday morning, we would come to the communion table of the Lord, not realizing that this "special bread" was always before the priests who ministered in the house of God. Now we, as Messianic Gentiles, can go back to our olive-tree roots and enjoy the richness of the sap that flows from the covenant to His people, Israel, and to those like us that have been grafted in by grace and mercy. We come into a place with the Lord on the Sabbath to have fellowship with Him and to remind ourselves that He is the Bread of Life that came down from heaven to give us life.

In Solomon's temple, the Levites were responsible for preparing, for every Sabbath, the bread set out on the table. 1 Samuel 21:2-6 "David answered Ahimelech the priest, 'The king charged me with a certain matter and said to me, "No one is to know anything about your mission and your instructions."' "As for my men, I have told them to meet me at a certain place. Now then, what do you have on hand? Give me five loaves of bread, or whatever you can find. But the priest answered David, 'I don't have any ordinary bread on hand; however, there is some consecrated bread here – provided the men have kept themselves from women.' David replied, 'Indeed women have been kept from us, as usual whenever I set out. The men's things are holy even on missions that are not holy. How much more so today!' So the priest gave him the consecrated bread, since there was no bread there except the bread of the Presence that had been removed from before the LORD and replaced by hot bread on the day it was taken away." The story of David is a picture of the bread of life sustaining us while the battle is on.

Five is the number for the Lord's grace in our lives. The Sabbath bread is His extended hand of grace to us through the generations. In the book of Matthew 12:1-8, we have the picture of Yeshua turning the disciples back to the book of Samuel. "At that time Jesus went through the grainfields on the Sabbath. His disciples were hungry and began to pick some heads of grain and eat them. When the Pharisees saw this, they said to him, 'Look! Your disciples are doing what is unlawful on the Sabbath'. He answered, 'Haven't you read what David did when he and his companions were hungry? He entered the house of God, and he and his companions ate the consecrated bread—which was not lawful for them to do, but only for the priests. Or haven't you read in the Law that on the Sabbath the priests in the temple desecrate the day and yet are innocent? I tell you that one greater than the temple is here. If you had known what these words mean, "I desire mercy, not sacrifice", you would not have condemned the innocent. For the Son of Man is Lord of the Sabbath.'"

We need to understand that Yeshua always pointed the disciples back to the foundation of the faith. And He has not stopped today. He still points the church, "The called out ones," to see the foundation that the Prophets of Old stood on. King David speaks through his actions and reveals the love of the Messiah to us today. Yeshua still points the church back and reveals that everything He did was for our benefit, to *understand that we are standing on the same, everlasting foundation that will never be moved. Yes, the times are modern, but His Word is everlasting, to the Jew first, and then to the Gentile.*

As a gift to us, God gave the symbol of the challah bread as a beautiful picture of the "Bread of Life"- Yeshua is His Name. "I am the bread of life. Your forefathers ate the manna in the desert, yet they died. But here is the bread that comes down from heaven, which a man may eat and not die. I am the living bread that came down from heaven. If anyone eats of this bread, he will live forever. This bread is my flesh, which I will give for the life of the world." John 6:48-51

Because we know that Yeshua observed the Sabbath and sat with His family to eat bread and drink from the cup, we can also enjoy our heritage in the Lord with an awareness of who the Bread of Life is. Even the two disciples on the road to Emmaus had their eyes opened as Yeshua blessed the bread with the Hebrew blessing. Their eyes were opened and they at once recognized Him as the Risen Messiah, the Bread of Life.

You may enjoy speaking the Hebrew Blessing over your challah bread, which is as follows; "Baruch Ata Adonai, Eloheinu Melech ha'Olam, hamotzi lechem min ha-aretz. Blessed are You, O Lord our God, King of the Universe, who brings forth bread from the earth." Shabbat Shalom, everyone!

Scriptures To Know And Store In Our Hearts:

Genesis 2:2-3 "By the seventh day God had finished the work he had been doing; so on the seventh day he rested from all his work. And God blessed the seventh day and made it holy, because on it he rested from all the work of creating that he had done."

1 Samuel 21:2-6 "David answered Ahimelech the priest, 'The king charged me with a certain matter and said to me, "No one is to know anything about your mission and your instructions."' As for my men, I have told them to meet me at a certain place. Now then, what do you have on hand? Give me five loaves of bread, or whatever you can find. But the priest answered David, "I don't have any ordinary bread on hand; however, there is some consecrated bread here – provided the men have kept themselves from women." David replied, "Indeed women have been kept from us, as usual whenever I set out. The men's things are holy even on missions that are not holy. How much more so today!" So the priest gave him the consecrated bread, since there was no bread there except the bread of the Presence that had been removed from before the LORD and replaced by hot bread on the day it was taken away."'

Matthew 12:1-8 "At that time Jesus went through the grainfields on the Sabbath. His disciples were hungry and began to pick some heads of grain and eat them. When the Pharisees saw this, they said to him, 'Look! Your disciples are doing what is unlawful on the Sabbath'. He answered, 'Haven't you read what David did when he and his companions were hungry? He entered the house of God, and he and his companions ate the consecrated bread—which was not lawful for them to do, but only for the priests. Or haven't you read in the Law that on the Sabbath the priests in the temple desecrate the day and yet are innocent? I tell you that one greater than the temple is here. If you had known what these words mean, 'I desire mercy, not sacrifice', you would not have condemned the innocent. For the Son of Man is Lord of the Sabbath."

John 6:48-51 "I am the bread of life. Your forefathers ate the manna in the desert, yet they died. But here is the bread that comes down from heaven, which a man may eat and not die. I am the living bread that came down from heaven. If anyone eats of this bread, he will live forever. This bread is my flesh, which I will give for the life of the world."

Luke 24:30-32 "When he was at the table with them, he took bread, gave thanks, broke it and began to give it to them. Then their eyes were opened and they recognized him, and he disappeared from their sight. They asked each other, 'Were not our hearts burning within us while he talked with us on the road and opened the Scriptures to us?'"

Prayer of Revelation:

Dear Abba,

Thank You for Your Son, the Bread of Life, whose Name is Yeshua. How our hearts are hungry, even as the disciples were hungry on the Sabbath. We ask that You feed us with Your very sustenance that we might live today and forevermore. We ask that as we come to Your Sabbath day of rest, that the sweet smelling challah bread would fill our homes with delight and joy. You came down from heaven as the Bread of Life so that we might live and taste and see that You are good.

B'shem Yeshua,

Amen.

Elisheva - The Abrahamic Covenant – The Brit

Elisheva was excited about the day ahead of her. She was invited to the "brit" of her eight-day-old nephew. On this day of celebration, her family would come from miles around to witness the event: her Aunt and Uncle from Shiloh, her cousin from Joppa, her brother and his wife from Beersheba, and her lovely Aunt Zipporah from Bethel. They would all ascend to the Temple today, in anticipation of the blessing from the Priest being placed upon their newest little family member. Her sister, Devorah, and Devorah's husband, Aaron, had looked forward to this day from the moment Devorah knew she was with child. They had secretly longed for a son, and Devorah knew she cradled one in her womb.

Elisheva's heart welled up with happiness for this sister of hers. Since she was a young girl, Devorah had feared that no one would find her attractive enough to want her as his bride. Then, to her delight, along came Aaron, and it truly was an Isaac and Rebekah type of love story. Aaron had caught a brief glimpse of Devorah in the market as she was buying vegetables for the evening meal, and he believed at first sight that she was the one God had sent him. But he knew that the process to have her as his wife would take time, and there was also the possibility that she would not have him. Happily, though, his hope became reality one year later as she stood beneath the Chuppah as his bride. He thought Devorah was the most beautiful woman in all of Jerusalem, and never once realized that his Devorah ever had deep insecurities about her looks. Her secret never had to be divulged.

Elisheva loved this beautiful story and others that she often thought about. They spoke to her of the faithfulness of her God that, no matter what, life continued on through His people, Israel.

She began to gather her belongings for the day's event: a basket of food, a small blanket for her nephew that she had purchased especially for the occasion, and her favorite shawl she always wore when going near the temple courts. Elisheva would meet her family in Solomon's courtyard. She would keep an eye out for her taller-than-average Uncle Oni from Shiloh. The family always teased Uncle Oni and would say that if you were ever lost in the desert, just look for Uncle Oni's wild, raven colored hair, and it would lead you back to the temple courts in Jerusalem!

This would be another of many "brit" Abrahamic covenant ceremonies that she had seen. But this one held a special excitement for Elisheva because this was the first one in her own family. As she approached Solomon's court, she was overwhelmed with the sights and sounds that came at her from every direction. The enormous temple stood majestically as a monument to her God. It seemed to touch the footstool of His throne in the heavens.

Elisheva, captivated by the awesome sight before her, did not hear her name being called. Coming toward her was Zipporah, her aunt from Bethel, waving her delicate hand. She so enjoyed her aunt Zipporah. She was named after Zipporah in the Holy Scrolls, Moshe's wife, who circumcised their son because Moshe had hesitated to do it. In one swift movement, she had taken the flint knife, performed the circumcision herself, and thrown the foreskin down at Moshe's feet. Now there was a woman of character!

And now her namesake, Elisheva's aunt, was also, in her own way, a woman of character. There was a strength in her that Elisheva hoped to one day have in herself. And even though she was strong, Aunt Zipporah's soft, lovely, womanhood radiated from every pore of her vessel, quite unconsciously. Elisheva was conscious of it, though, and admired her graceful, beautiful aunt, who, even at her age, turned heads as they looked upon her beauty.

As she had readied herself today, Elisheva couldn't shake the feeling that something would happen today that would change her life. What silly thoughts she was thinking. She looked forward to every day that God gave her and she loved to find the treasures hidden in each one, but today she felt something different. The anticipation was palpable as Elisheva laid her hand upon her heart, feeling the rhythm of it beating faster than normal. What would happen today? What would she see? Whatever the events of the day held, Elisheva decided that the very best part would be the fulfillment of the dedication of little Shmuel's life as he would be presented to the Lord, for it is written in the law, "Every firstborn male is to be consecrated to Adonai."

When the God of heaven had visited Abram, He changed his name to Abraham. And then He gave Abraham this command – for the Hebrew people to circumcise every male child on the eighth day. To this very day, every God-fearing Jewish couple eagerly counted the days to this event for their sons. Today was her nephew's day to experience this reenactment of obedience before the God of Israel.

As a handmaiden who loved her people and her God, Elisheva felt privileged, even in this modern day, to see it. She knew that every male baby of Israel was to undergo circumcision, and that it was a sign of the covenant between God and her people, Israel. This was to take place on precisely the eighth day – not the seventh, not the ninth – but the eighth day. The joy and excitement was electrifying for each and every member of the family who would witness this ancient act. Elisheva had heard that this ritual was to be observed, not only by her people, Israel, but also by Gentiles who had converted to the God of Israel and His ways. She rejoiced at how wonderful her God was to those who had chosen to come out of darkness, that He showed His love to them by bringing them into His family, also.

At last, everyone was assembled in the courts of Yahweh. The songs of blessings began as a reminder of what their God had given to Abram on the day his name was changed. And on this, the eighth day of his life, her nephew would finally be given his name. She could hardly wait to find out what name Devorah and Aaron had "selected" for their first-born son. She knew that it would be the name that their God had spoken over this child from before the foundations of the earth. It was a mystery how He saw to it that each child received the name that He had ordained for His purposes in every generation.

She saw the sharp instrument that was used in the cutting off of the foreskin. She looked at her sister and her proud brother-in-law standing so stately before the priest with their precious son. Quickly, before anyone had time to catch his or her breath, it was done. Her nephew was lifted upward as a new life into the household of Israel. He was wrapped in swaddling linen cloth and was given to the purposes of Yahweh. She saw the priest give the baby to Aaron with an outstretched hand of authority. The name Shmuel was laid upon him as a garment that he would wear forever. The ancient hour that came upon Abraham had entered into the courts again today. Elisheva felt as though Abraham, Isaac and Jacob had been looking on with approval.

Out of the corner of her eye, something caught Elisheva's attention. She looked closer and realized that another brit ceremony was taking place in the court. There was a sense of holiness about this baby boy who was brought to fulfill the law of God. What was it about this baby just a few feet away that seemed so different from little Shmuel? She was straining to get a closer look when she heard his name pronounced. They named him Yeshua.

Time seemed to stand still in Solomon's temple. Elisheva could not believe what she was witnessing and what affect this family was having on her. She did not know why she began trembling inside and had not even been aware that Shmuel had already made known the discomfort that the sharp flint knife had inflicted. The sound of his cries echoed through the temple courts, mingling with the cries of the other sons of the covenant, filling the space of eternity.

Little Shmuel was so lovingly held in his father's arms. Aaron had always been sweet and kind to Devorah, but even more so since the baby. The love that flowed through their eyes to each other sometimes took Elisheva's breath away as she, too, longed for that same kind of love and a family of her own one day. The beauty of seeing Aaron, a father, hold his first-born son was a picture of the eternal covenant of God's love to His people, Israel. How thankful Elisheva felt to be a part of His family and to know that she would also have the opportunity to see many more "brits" in her lifetime. And she looked forward to the day that she would hold little Shmuel on her lap and recount the events of this day to him. Elisheva would be a wonderful aunt and couldn't wait to be called "Doda" by her precious nephew.

Later that evening, Elisheva sat in her comfortable little home reflecting on the day's events. Her mind's eye kept seeing the other baby, whose name she heard was Yeshua, being circumcised today alongside Shmuel. The look upon the face of the mother who held this child was so beautiful. She was glowing from within, and the glow radiated from her lovely face. The husband touched this lovely woman's sleeve and said, "Miriam, our son is special." Those words, Elisheva felt, had a secret meaning that only the two of them understood. Yes, of course, Elisheva understood that every parent thought his child was the most beautiful of all, but still, she sensed that there really was something very special that she, too, felt about this baby named Yeshua.

Thoughts To Meditate On:

What does this beautiful ceremony mean to us today as Messianic Gentile believers? We have knowledge through the scriptures that Yeshua was circumcised on the eighth day and that is when He received the name, Yeshua. Our Jewish brothers and sisters celebrate what is called Simchah Torah, rejoicing in the Torah, or in modern terms, rejoicing in the instructions of God's Words. Joseph and Miriam brought Yeshua into the courts of the Lord to have Him circumcised like every other eight-day-old Jewish baby boy.

Let's go back to our bedrock and find out what was spoken through the prophets and how it is important for you and me to have this "brit" ceremony take place in our own hearts. The prophet Jeremiah said in Jeremiah 4:4 "Circumcise yourselves to the LORD, circumcise your hearts, you men of Judah and people of Jerusalem, or my wrath will break out and burn like fire because of the evil you have done—burn with no one to quench it."

We have the responsibility to observe this command ourselves in this hour. This is not just an "Old Testament" command - it is a command of the Lord to us today. Colossians 2:11-12 says, " In him you were also circumcised, in the putting off of the sinful nature, not with a circumcision done by the hands of men but with the circumcision done by Christ, having been buried with him in baptism and raised with him through your faith in the power of God, who raised him from the dead."

We must remember that what we see in the "New Testament" is a reflection of what was spoken in the "Old Testament." Even in this era, all over the world Jewish people are circumcising their sons on the eighth day to separate them from the effects of the world around them and to set them apart unto the Lord. As we give our hearts to be circumcised by the Ruach HaKodesh to cut away the hold of the world on us, we become set apart for the Lord's purposes.

We must understand the seriousness of this Covenant act. We have heard about the story of Exodus 4:25 when Zipporah, one of Moses' wives, had to take a stand, even in front of her husband Moses, and cut the foreskin off of her own son with a flint knife. Without the cutting away of the world, we will not be able to walk in the paths of righteousness. We will still be part of the world, and it will have ownership over us. The Lord gave this word in John 15:19 "If you belonged to the world, it would love you as its own. As it is, you do not belong to the world, but I have chosen you out of the world. That is why the worlds hates you."

I thank my Jewish brothers and sisters for the outward ceremony that we, as Messianic Gentiles, have the privilege to witness to remind us that we ourselves, who have come as foreigners, need to continually have the foreskin of our hearts cut away so that we can live before Him with openness of devotion.

Scriptures To Know And Store In Our Hearts:

Genesis 17:9-14 "God said to Abraham, 'As for you, you are to keep my covenant, you and your descendants after you, generation after generation. Here is my covenant, which you are to keep, between me and you, along with your descendants after you: every male among you is to be circumcised. You are to be circumcised in the flesh of your foreskin; this will be the sign of the covenant between me and you. Generation after generation, every male among you who is eight days old is to be circumcised, including slaves born within your household and those bought from a foreigner not descended from you. The slave born in your house and the person bought with your money must be circumcised; thus my covenant will be in your flesh as an everlasting covenant. Any uncircumcised male who will not let himself be circumcised in the flesh of his foreskin – that person will be cut off from his people, because he has broken my covenant.'" CJB*

Jeremiah 4:4 "Circumcise yourselves to the LORD, circumcise your hearts, you men of Judah and people of Jerusalem, or my wrath will break out and burn like fire because of the evil you have done— burn with no one to quench it."

Exodus 4:25 "But Zipporah took a flint knife, cut off her son's foreskin and touched Moses' feet with it. 'Surely you are a bridegroom of blood to me,' she said."

Deuteronomy 10:16-21 "Circumcise your hearts, therefore, and do not be stiff-necked any longer. For the LORD your God is God of gods and Lord of lords, the great God, mighty and awesome, who shows no partiality and accepts no bribes. He defends the cause of the fatherless and the widow, and loves the alien, giving him food and clothing. And you are to love those who are aliens, for you yourselves were aliens in Egypt. Fear the LORD your God and serve him. Hold fast to him and take your oaths in his name. He is your praise; he is your God, who performed for you those great and awesome wonders you saw with your own eyes."

Deuteronomy 30:6 "The LORD your God will circumcise your hearts and the hearts of your descendants, so that you may love him *with all your heart and with all your soul, and live."*

<u>Romans 2:28-29</u> *"A man is not a Jew if he is only one outwardly, nor is circumcision merely outward and physical. No, a man is a Jew if he is one inwardly; and circumcision is circumcision of the heart, by the Spirit, not by the written code. Such a man's praise is not from men, but from God."*

<u>Colossians 2:9-13</u> *"For in him, bodily, lives the fullness of all that God is. And it is in union with him that you have been made full – he is the head of every rule and authority.*

Also it was in union with him that you were circumcised with a circumcision not done by human hands, but accomplished by stripping away the old nature's control over the body. In this circumcision done by the Messiah, you were buried along with him by being immersed; and in union with him, you were also raised up along with him by God's faithfulness that worked when he raised Yeshua from the dead. You were dead because of your sins, that is, because your 'foreskin,' your old nature. But God made you alive along with the Messiah by forgiving you all your sins." CJB

Prayer of Revelation:

Abba Father,

How thankful we are to witness in this day your people abiding in Your everlasting covenant by circumcising their baby sons on the eighth day. And how thankful I am that Your Apostles wrote to us about Yeshua's parents fulfilling the law of circumcision over Your Son, Yeshua, and that we must today fulfill it in our hearts. It is, once more, a sign that we, as Messianic Gentiles, are grafted into the Olive Tree of your people, Israel. Please circumcise our hearts and cut away any anti-Semitic spirit that would entrap our hearts not to love Your people, Israel.

I pray this in Yeshua's name,

Amen.

Yael - The New Moon

Yael could not sleep this night as she paced back and forth across her cool stone floor. Why was she not like the other young handmaidens fast asleep without a care in the world? She was so tired of the endless chatter about what new fabric had just arrived in Jerusalem or the gossip about the new tenants that had arrived from Bethany.

Opening her door, Yael knew she was searching for truth that would fill her empty heart. Yes, she, like any handmaiden, desired to have the perfect husband standing beside her under the chuppah that marked a marriage covenant between man and woman. She, too, longed for children to be brought forth from her womb. And yet Yael knew an even deeper longing that was far past all the natural longings, and that was to know her God. Yes, the same Mighty God that delivered her people and brought them into this land where her own bare feet were now standing.

She pondered the night sky, and to her amazement, the New Moon was speaking to her, "I have a secret to share. Will you listen?" She shook her head and figured she was just imagining things. Why was she so fascinated with the New Moon that appeared every month, faithfully on time, to announce to her and all of Israel, "Something is about to break forth into your earthly atmosphere. Are you ready?" The New Moon always brought a spirit of expectation to her people. It marked new beginnings, new horizons, new truths, new awareness, and it was a reminder of the signs and seasons that God gave to her people throughout the generations.

As a young girl, she had heard that at the beginning of the Torah scrolls it was written, "And God said, 'Let there be lights in the expanse of the sky to separate the day from the night, and let them serve as signs to mark seasons and days and years, and let them be lights in the expanse of the sky to give light on the earth.' And it was so. God made two great lights—the greater light to govern the day and the lesser light to govern the night. He also made the stars."

As she again contemplated the night-portrait that was created by her God, she took comfort in knowing that those who seek Him will find Him. What news was the New Moon going to speak to her in this hour of her life? She hoped it was the answer to her yearning. But how could she seek these answers? Where could she go, since she was a woman, to ask such questions about the New Moon? Who would even care that she wanted to learn of the deep mysteries of the ancient scrolls? But she believed that somehow God would show her.

The intoxicating smell of jasmine jolted Yael back to her whereabouts and she became aware that every part of her body was coming alive. And she knew that what was happening to her was holy and that no one could say it was unclean. Was this what the appearing of the New Moon was trying to do to awaken her people to the appearance of the Messiah?

She had experienced this awakening before. It brought such a strong sense of longing for Him herself. Not just a longing for the Messiah to come as the prophets said He would come for her people, but a longing because she knew He would come for her. She had such a deep confidence within her that He saw her and loved her and was coming for her.

Yael breathed in the rich, thick smell of love in the air and knew in that moment she had captured it. This love she knew that came from her God had waited for this season to come and lead her people into their destiny of being different from all the other people that surrounded this holy land. Out loud, Yael heard herself say, "New Moon, speak forth the truths that you have carried from the moment our God brought you forth into the heavens."

Tomorrow, Yael would go to Uncle Obed's village to see him. He was a delightful, elderly man who had gained much wisdom over his many decades. She smiled to herself, knowing that he would at least listen to her yearning and could hopefully assist her in his gentle way.

Donning her beautiful veil of deep purple, she tried to control her steps as she hurriedly left her home, with a deep sense that something was about to happen. It was like walking around a bend in the road and coming into the brightness of the morning sun and seeing its first rays skip across the Judean mountains, playing with the landscape.

Oh, how she desired to know the mysteries of life and the Creator of life. She had knowledge in her mind of Him, but her heart was aching to know the One who spoke life into Adam's body. She knew her people were special, but, really, why? Why were they called out of Egypt to live in this land to be different? What was the purpose? She knew her people were waiting for the Messiah. There was always talk in the villages around the Temple, but yet no one had seen the One that the prophets spoke about. Oh, she had recently heard another rumor about someone from Nazareth, but it soon died out because everyone knew who his parents were.

The nearby village of Bethlehem was the home of her Uncle Obed and his wife, Yehudit. The abundance of love in their household was always a gift to Yael, but never more than at this time in her life. She was between seasons. Some would say she was young, but then others would say she was touching the undesirable age, passing the most acceptable season for marriage. She was thankful that her Uncle and Aunt loved her at any age, and welcomed her any time of the day or night.

Her Uncle's wisdom was well known and many people from the surrounding areas came to seek her uncle's advice on life's challenges. Some would say he was a Torah scholar. All Yael knew for certain was that her uncle was a man who loved God with all his heart, mind and soul. He seemed to have the same love for God that the holy scroll said about King David, who also had a willing heart to serve their God. But more than a just a willing heart, David gave his whole heart to God and almost seemed to have a personal relationship with Him. King David wrote as though he actually saw the Holy One of Israel and talked to Him as a man would talk to his best friend. His writings exposed his inner frustrations, but always ended in praise to his God.

Her Uncle Obed was exactly the same way, and Yael desired that kind of relationship, too. She noticed that her Uncle talked as though the Messiah could just walk right into his home and sit down and have a glass of Sabbath wine with him. Could this actually happen? Would the Messiah sit under the New Moon and teach her people about the wonders of the Eternal Kingdom? Would He touch the outcast as her prophets said He would do and wash their filth away?

Yael found herself constantly asking these questions and actually waiting for Someone to answer her. She longed for a personal relationship with the Unseen God who displayed His love to her people by delivering them from all of the raging enemies that surrounded them but was only seen in the signs and wonders displayed before them. Oh yes, she knew of the pillar of fire by day, the cloud by night, the manna that fell from heaven, the water from the rock, the sandals that never wore out on her forefathers' feet, and most of all, the Shekinah that was seen by all her people as they stood outside the tent of meeting. So many signs her God gave to her people to draw them into His presence, and most of all, to know Him.

The Holy Scrolls taught that He was eternal and that there was no beginning and no end to Him. The writings say He is the Aleph and the Tav, the beginning of the alphabet and the end. Every Hebrew child knew that the alphabet of their language was eternal. It was a picture of the full moon, no beginning to the starting point of the circle and no end. How magnificent is the God of her people!

As she tarried by the well that held sweet water for the inhabitants of Bethlehem, she looked at the humble state of this village. Again, she felt that something wonderful had happened in this little village but had not as yet made its existence known to the people. The prophet Isaiah had spoken about the Messiah and the place that He would be brought forth. But was it to be in her day or in the days ahead when she would already be gathered to her fathers? This, she did not know.

Peering into the water's edge, she saw the silhouette of her face, softened by the water caressing the reflection of her skin. Is that really what she looked like immersed in the water? She looked like a newborn with the kiss of God's approval. Did God approve of her desire to know Him? Deep inside, she believed He did, but as always, the reassurance from her uncle's mouth kept her heart secure.

Arriving at her Uncle and Aunt's house, Yael was greeted by the lovely singing of her Aunt Yehudit. It was the sound of a sweet love song being lifted up as an offering to Yahweh. She heard, coming from her Aunt's very soul, a yearning in each word that was expressed to the Invisible God of her people. "Yahweh, we wait in the words You have spoken through Your prophets that You will send a Messiah to come and deliver us. We wait as a wife waits for her husband to enter her bedchamber of delight. We have oiled our bodies, perfumed ourselves, and put on our finest garments to welcome Him. As the New Moon reminds us that You are gathering Your people to Your Holy Mountain to meet You, Messiah, we will continue to raise an offering of thankfulness to Your Name, Yahweh. From One New Moon to the next, we will come and bow down before you with adoration." Yael's heart began to swell with passion as she heard these words fill their humble dwelling.

Her Aunt Yehudit turned and saw Yael, and with her usual squeal of delight, reached and gave her a huge hug. For Yael, it felt so good to be in the arms of someone who loved her "just because" and she could feel flesh and blood against her. As much as she adored them, the reality was she ached to be held by someone other than her Uncle and Aunt. She ached, not only to be held by the Messiah, but also to be held by the one man He would send to come and love her with all that was in him.

Her Uncle Obed arrived, and the scene repeated itself. Yael began to ask her uncle questions concerning the coming of the Messiah. She was aware that no one really knew the exact time, but that the righteous were always waiting with total confidence that "He would come." And the realization finally hit her that the expectation of her people for the coming of the Messiah was actually binding them together, as a people, in one heart and one mind.

After much eating and much talking, Yael reluctantly decided it was time that she left for home. It surprised her that the night had arrived, yet her heart was filled with the brightness of the sun, as though she were walking into the light of day. More kissing, and then she turned down the worn path which had caressed so many sandals before her. Smelling the jasmine mingled with the honeysuckle, she threw her head back to fully breathe in the aroma of pure delight. As she opened her eyes, she again beheld in the night sky the sign of promise, the New Moon.

Coming through the corridors that led to her small dwelling, she heard much laughter and gaiety, and was drawn to the sound as a bee to a flower. She followed the joy path. There she looked into an open door and saw the most exquisite looking Man - not a Man with classic handsomeness, but with ancient, yet timeless features etched by an Artist who knew this was His finest piece of beauty. This Man was surrounded by at least twelve others who were attentive to every word that came forth from His mouth. She knew she was an intruder, but somehow felt welcomed into His words and not shunned because she was a woman.

With no chance for her to hide behind the open door, He looked up and His love entered her heart with a flaming arrow of fire. Her entire body began to burn with a fire that she had never experienced in her life. She felt clean and whole from the inside out and not ashamed of her love for this One who cleansed her with the fire from His eyes. At once, she realized that the New Moon had been speaking to her, "He is here. The Messiah is here, and you will seek Him with all your heart and you will find Him amongst your people." Yael knew that all her desires were met in a single glance, and He knew her as though she were His bride.

Thoughts To Meditate On:

It is difficult for us, as non-Jews, to figure out what the New Moon has to do with us today, as the church. I must challenge you that just because we cannot understand something, we must not give in to the tendency to push it aside.

What can we learn from the scriptures concerning the New Moon? I know personally that every time I look up into the night sky and see the New moon appearing, I now have a full month to expand in the knowledge of the Lord. I hunger and thirst with intensity for the revelation that the Ruach HaKodesh so freely gives as I ask of Him. I desire more understanding of the hour we are in and of the eternal covenant to His people, Israel, and to myself as a wild olive branch grafted into their Olive Tree.

The new moon is a sign, not only to Israel, but also to those of us who believe in the covenant God, that He will not break His word, nor will His word come back void, but it will come to pass in the fullness of time, even as He speaks and the New Moon begins to grow to its fullness every month. As it expands, The New Moon becomes the stamp from a signet ring on the hand of Yahweh. He has declared that the heavens, the earth, and all that is below belong to Him. He has sealed His covenant with His people Israel and with all of those who have been grafted into His family.

Scriptures To Know And Store In Our Hearts:

<u>Genesis 1:14-18</u> *"And God said, 'Let there be lights in the expanse of the sky to separate the day from the night, and let them serve as signs to mark seasons and days and years, and let them be lights in the*

expanse of the sky to give light on the earth.' And it was so. God made two great lights—the greater light to govern the day and the lesser light to govern the night. He also made the stars. God set them in the expanse of the sky to give light on the earth, to govern the day and the night, and to separate light from darkness. And God saw that it was good. And there was evening, and there was morning—the fourth day."

Numbers 10:10 "Also at your times of rejoicing—your appointed feasts and New Moon festivals—you are to sound the trumpets over your burnt offerings and fellowship offerings, and they will be a memorial for you before your God. I am the LORD your God."

1 Samuel 20:5 "So David said, "Look, tomorrow is the New Moon festival, and I am supposed to dine with the king; but let me go and hide in the field until the evening of the day after tomorrow."

Psalm 81:3-5 "Sound the ram's horn at the New Moon, and when the moon is full, on the day of our Feast; this is a decree for Israel, an ordinance of the God of Jacob. He established it as a statute for Joseph when he went out against Egypt, where we heard a language we did not understand."

Isaiah 66:23 "'From one New Moon to another and from one Sabbath to another, all mankind will come and bow down before me,' says the LORD."

Jeremiah 31:35-36 "This is what the LORD says, he who appoints the sun to shine by day, who decrees the moon and stars to shine by night, who stirs up the sea so that its waves roar—the LORD Almighty is his name: 'Only if these decrees vanish from my sight,' declares the LORD, 'will the descendants of Israel ever cease to be a nation before me.'"

Ezekiel 46:1 "This is what the Sovereign LORD says: The gate of the inner court facing east is to be shut on the six working days, but on the Sabbath day and on the day of the New Moon it is to be opened."

Ezekiel 46:3 "On the Sabbaths and New Moons the people of the land are to worship in the presence of the LORD at the entrance to that gateway."

Prayer of Revelation:

Dear Abba, Father,

Reveal to us the truth of the New Moon. Give light to the eyes of our understanding, that we may begin every New Moon with a fresh awareness and be reminded of Your faithfulness to expand within us. We ask, Abba, that the fullness of Your glory be seen in us as we walk through the streets of our nations to touch the people that You have created to come to the knowledge of the precious gift of Your Son, Yeshua. Lord, our heart is to identify with Your people Israel – not to remain as foreigners among them.

We make this request because we know that You hear us as we call out the Name of Your Son, Yeshua.

Amen.

Rivkah – The Tear Bottle

Rivkah was struggling this morning with just life. She felt overwhelmed by the many chores she had to do on this day and the many people who depended on her for their happiness. Her husband Reuben was a good man, but did he understand her heart and what she felt like today? Her children brought so much joy to her even as she thought about their smiling faces looking upward to her for a bite of sweet bread. So why did she feel like crying? Why did her heart want to reach out to someone who would understand her tears and who would not question her and would tell her she would be all right and that this would all pass soon? Where was that person in her life? Did that person exist? One day she would find that one Person who would understand her emotions and sympathize with her. Over what, she did not know, but that Person would understand and be there for her without questioning her thoughts about life.

Her good friend Anat was constantly telling her she should drink some special blend of herbal tea that was supposed to have a "calming effect." Rivkah always found a way to conceal her look of disdain as she tried to refrain from imagining the smell of such a concoction, without even having a cup in front of her. She knew her friend Anat meant well, but a cup of disgusting tea was not going to heal the ache in her heart. Anat had told her of a popular herbal shop in their village who carried it. But Rivkah knew that the shop was successful because they merchandised off of everyone's aches and pains. In reality, most of the aches and pains were not on the outside, but on the inside. Of course, the shopkeeper knew he did not have the cure for the inside, but he was quite happy to sell his merchandise to anyone who had good shekels in his or her coin pouch, anyway.

One thing she found at another shop that did she love, however, was a beautiful hand-made soap. It made her feel very womanly, and it did seem to wash away her despair for a time. But slowly, the lovely fragrance would fade away from her delicate skin, and her daydreams of being satisfied would dissipate along with it.

She often wondered how the women of her people of long ago dealt with their inward emotions. How did Sarah deal with the pain of being childless for so many years and seeing her handmaiden, Hagar, bear Abraham a child?

How did Rachel feel when her very own sister was given to the love of her life, Jacob, sleeping with him on what was supposed to be her own wedding night, while Rachel slept alone, her insides aching with the fire of passion, yet waking unsatisfied as a woman?

How did Abigail lie beside a man that everyone called a fool and submit to her wifely duty, letting him release his manhood into her beautiful vessel, knowing that he did not care about the heart within it?

How did Tamar feel when Judah's two sons died before giving her the child she desired to be formed within her womb, and then dressed herself as a prostitute to receive the semen of her two dead husbands' father, Judah? As she lay there knowing that she was falling in love with this man named Judah as the weight of his body was upon her, she also knew he could hate her for the way she chose to receive what was due her from his family line. Tamar knew that it was only the justice of the Law of Israel that would protect her from being stoned.

Rivkah knew the story of Rahab, the prostitute, who saved the two spies in Jericho. She stood with people of the God of Israel and later became the wife of one of them. How she must have endured the whispers of other women in the tribes that said she would never be a true Israelite. Rivkah knew in her heart that Rahab must have shed many tears of pain, as well as tears of joy, as she lay beside her new husband who took her as part of his soul.

Then there was Bathsheba, who lost a husband as a result of the cunning act of King David to have her as his own. Bathsheba, as a woman, must have wept with sorrow for her lost husband as he gave his blood in battle, but she also must have wept because of her love for a King who desired her and her heart.

Rivkah concluded that the tears of a woman were powerful, indeed, and that her God had reached down from His throne to catch every drop from every woman's eyes through the ages and gathered them back to Himself. She knew that the God who created woman also created the tears of a woman to refresh the hardened soil of her heart as she survived the atmosphere of hardship every day. She knew that somehow she was to be thankful for the tears that fell from her eyes, and that someday, they would produce a harvest of joy that would spring up from the earth of her own heart.

Many tears were shed because of the injustices to her ancestors, but yet in the end, the God of Abraham, Isaac and Jacob reached down and demanded justice for each and every one of these women. Would He reach down and demand justice for a woman such as herself who has not been written of in the Most Holy scrolls? Would the God that she loved care about her most-needed womanly desire – to live with joy, not only on the outside, but also on the inside of her body where the blood pumps and feeds her body to live? She desired this blood to also feed her soul and the chambers of her heart. Desire arose in her as she knew that her God would be faithful to send someone to her and to touch the very core of who she was. Before she took her last breath of life, she believed He would be faithful to her heart.

Rivkah decided to take a few minutes for herself and go to her secret place and sit beneath the palm tree that sheltered her and swayed in the gentle breeze of day. Before she knew it, she had fallen into a deep sleep by the soft touch of the wind. Feeling the warmth of the sun and the softness of the ground beneath her, she saw herself being given a beautiful bottle. In her dream, she accepted the gift and realized that her tears were being welcomed into this beautiful bottle. One by one, her tears of yesterday were filling this beautiful, ornate object. Now she also was seeing this morning's tears falling softly into the delicate vessel. With loving caresses, the bottle accepted her innermost wellspring into its chamber.

She thought to herself that someone must own this bottle, but Who? Why would someone care about her tears? Who would give her such a beautiful bottle to hold her tears? Looking to the hand that was holding this bottle, she beheld a Man robed in such whiteness that she saw herself shielding her eyes. She could not see the Man's face clearly, but she viewed the outline of the firmness of His jaw. She decided it was a face of strength, but yet tenderness was etched in lines that seemed to speak of wisdom that only comes with age. Silently, in her dream, she thought to herself that He was young, but possessed the wisdom that is aged with time.

To her surprise, she saw His tears falling into the same bottle that held her own, and they became one with the tears of sorrow and pain of her heart. Peace began to invade her being as she soon realized in her dream that He understood her fears and did not seem to scold her. He understood the loneliness she felt, even though she was surrounded by so many people who loved her, but who were always pulling on her to give them life. Who was the Man of white that held this tear bottle? Why would He care about her tears? She woke up.

So young in age, yet with so many people relying on her to make the surroundings enjoyable and fill the atmosphere with joy. Rivkah understood, as she looked around her dwelling, that she lived in a modest house, yet to the beggars outside the walls of Jerusalem, it was a house of means. She knew that, in their eyes, she was a woman of wealth and luxury with an abundance that spilled over her table each time she set food before her family.

There was a certain beggar at the city gates who always caught her eye, and she longed to reach out her hand to touch him and to somehow release the loneliness she saw deep in his soul. He was a lame man, but it wasn't the lameness that caused the pain she saw in his eyes. It was that he knew he would never be included in the multitude to go to the temple to bring his offering to the God of Israel.

Reuben always caught her before she reached this beggar man's hand and gave her a stern look of disapproval. She could not begin to even think about trying to tell her husband that she recognized the man's loneliness, and that the same abandoned look of despair in his eyes is what she felt in her own heart.

She so struggled with these thoughts and would usually try to argue with herself that she must soon be coming into her monthly cycle. But today, that argument would not work. She was not entering into the time of separation from her husband, but into the time of coming together with him, as the season of cleanliness was upon her after her mikveh bath. She knew it was required of a wife to be joyful as the two become one and the secrets of the woman flow into the chambers of the man, as, in turn, the man releases his life into the woman. It was such a mystery of God's plan, for the two separate bodies to become one.

Hurrying home, Rivkah entered her dwelling with a new awareness of thankfulness as she felt the warmth of the modest decorations that Reuben would bring home to her after bartering with his friends in the city. Reuben was a man who was well-liked and well-respected by all those who knew him. He had a small enterprise that offered the best intricate pottery vessels that could be purchased – not for ordinary use, but only for display in the rich homes of the city. Rich men always wanted others to see that they could afford frivolous merchandise that was not needed for the routine chores of the home – things that were good for no practical purpose at all except to speak of the wealth of their owners. Pieces that said to each guest, "You have now entered the home of a rich man."

Reuben had employed fine artisans and gave them a fair wage for the excellent work they produced. And Reuben himself was an admirable provider for his family's needs. Rivkah and the children were afforded an excellent lifestyle due to his exceptional business ways. There was always enough for every aspect of their lives. As a father to his children, there was none better. And as a husband to Rivkah, he gave an abundance in every way he could.

But there was an emptiness in her that Reuben did not know how to fulfill, and Rivkah could not find the words to express her need. Many times, as they lay in the night hours with hushed voices so as not to wake the children, she would try the best she could to explain that something was missing, yet always stopped short of the full truth so as not to damage his manliness. Yes, at times, their lovemaking was sweet, and he was tender to her, as a godly husband. But more and more, as she would lie there listening to the contented breathing pattern of Reuben, which always indicated his deep sleep had come, her tears would begin once again to fall into her feathered pillow. There had been a few times, during the last few years of feeling alone, that he had rolled over and asked her if she was crying. Of course, her response was always the same, "No, I must be coming down with a cold. I will be fine in the morning."

Each time she repeated these words to Reuben, she did wonder if other women in the village had ever spoken the same words to their husbands. Was she the only one who had longed and questioned the wanting in a woman's soul? Were not Jewish women the other half of the Israeli population? It took a man and a woman to make a whole nation, is that not so, she thought to herself? How could Israel expand without the womb and its gift as a shelter from the elements of the world during the baby's growing time? Was not Deborah, the prophetess, called a "mother of Israel"? A mother could not breast feed her baby without drawing the child close to her breast filled with milk. She knew, as one who had nursed her babies, that even as she heard the cry of longing from her baby, her milk would begin to release. Israeli women gave life and produced offspring that grew in their chosen wombs. Even she knew that the God of Israel had held their wombs as the treasure box, which in turn, held His creation of life. Little lives with needs and wants, whether male or female, would cry out for the touch of a warm hand or the warmth of liquid from a source that they could not yet understand but which made them feel safe and secure.

The beautiful, sleek, female cat that had adopted Rivkah's family as her owners, gave birth to a litter of kittens. Rivkah and the children watched as eager, young kittens pawed their mother's glands to release the flow of milk into their waiting stomachs, easing the cravings of their little, unsatisfied bellies. It was then that Rivkah realized that being a mother and a wife was, in fact, the same – to always fill the hunger in a wanting soul. But now she felt it was her turn to receive what she was craving, but it could not come from Reuben or her children. She finally realized it, confessed it, and released her expectations – especially from Reuben. True satisfaction would have to come from another source.

The day had begun with the usual duties for any mother and wife in Israel. As she heard the morning song of the doves, Rivkah breathed in the new day and believed again that the God of Israel was a wonderful, faithful God of His Word to her and her people. She was determined to enjoy herself and to try to get on with the life that had been given her to walk out before her husband, children and her people Israel.

That evening, just before her eyes closed for the night, Reuben informed her that he wanted her to come with him to the temple the next day. He had a question for one of the attending priests concerning a dispute he'd had with a customer who wanted to return a piece of pottery, claiming it was flawed. Reuben knew that it was not the piece of exquisite pottery that had a flaw, but that it was the owner who had the character flaw of overspending to indulge his fleshly desire to impress his wife's family who were here for a visit. The man was in need of money, but had not been honest in his dealings with Reuben and had caused some whispers against Reuben's character and his business practices. Reuben wanted to seek the Godly counsel of the attending priest so he could deal with this incident in a way that would bring the most peaceful result to both parties involved.

Rivkah was excited just to know that she would be able to

break the routine of her everyday life. Her husband needed to have her with him, but of course, he could not let on that he really did depend on her for this kind of emotional support. He had to be careful before the men of the community and could not show his dependency on her in public. If he did, it would make it difficult for other men who would never let on that they needed their wives, not only for physical fulfillment, but for emotional fulfillment as well. There were very few men who could ever admit this, even to their closest male companions.

With each step toward their destination on the Temple Mount, the atmosphere became more and more alive because of the Holy God on the Mountain. Rivkah loved it when Reuben chose to enter through the Sheep's Gate because of all the excitement and the variety of people who came there from every walk of life. She recognized the stones, worn down by the sandaled feet of her people who were dedicated to the Words of their forefathers. So many had come and gone, but those who held the truth of the Torah Scrolls would pass on to new listeners the legacy of the Words of Eternal Life that called them to be a nation of priests. There was one thing about their prophets – they offered this message to every tongue, tribe, and nation who would receive these seeds of light into their hearts and let them grow. The God of Israel freely gave His Word to all peoples to wear upon their own hearts.

Rivkah and her husband neared the Pool of Bethesda, which was covered by five colonnades, magnificent in appearance. She couldn't help but think about a young Jewish woman named Hadassah who lived in a palace and was the joint hero with her uncle Mordecai in saving their people from extinction. She often wondered what it was like for Hadassah to live amongst carved pillars and to wear beautiful silk gowns woven to perfectly fit her young body. Rivkah pretended to be royalty and was again thankful that she had lovely garments to wear, perfectly tailored by her own hand, a skill her awkward young fingers had finally perfected after years of her mother's instruction which prepared her for marriage.

Today, around the pool, so many waited for evidence of the

supernatural story that was passed down through word of mouth that an angel of the Lord would come down and stir the waters which would produce a healing for the one who got in first. The disabled, blind, lame, and paralyzed were brought by family members to obtain a sense of hope, both for the person and for the family members who looked upon their hopeless bodies. What Rivkah came to realize was that all of them were hopeless, whether they walked or not. The walking family members felt the pain of guilt, just as the ones who laid limp felt the pain of their useless limbs. Where was the One who would heal all who were paralyzed, not only in their legs, but in their hearts? Rivkah herself felt paralytic in her heart, yet her legs could move freely.

Reuben always walked briskly past this pool because it made him feel uncomfortable to see those who did not have his way of life. He felt that if he did not see it, he would not have to respond to it. And, Rivkah, at one time, honestly felt the same way until that first day she looked into the beggar man's eyes at the Jaffa Gate and recognized herself. Eyes of loneliness and despair that questioned life's injustices.

All of a sudden, she saw a Rabbi talking to a lame man, and the air around the lame man seemed to be ignited with fire and light. She overheard the Rabbi say, "Do you want to get well?" Rivkah stopped short and did not even realize that Reuben had walked on, thinking she was at his side, as always. "Of course," her own voice blurted out loud for the lame man in response to the Rabbi. Then she heard the lame man give an explanation of why he had not gotten into the water to be healed. She wanted to scream and say to the lame man, "Listen, your answer will come from the piercing words of the Rabbi."

With a clear sound as loud as a ram's horn that sounds the wake up call to come to the mountain to worship the Holy God, the Rabbi said, "Get up, pick up your mat and walk." Rivkah held her breath for the whole crowd, which seemed to capture the scene in a motionless pause in eternity, as they all waited for what would happen next. Suddenly, as if someone started the world in motion again, the lame man stood up! Rivkah felt the warmth of tears flowing down her cheeks, which also seemed to wash over her heart with fire. She welcomed the feeling, for it quenched the yearning she had for so long for her insides to come alive in just such away. She saw tears of rejoicing erupt from the once lame man, now a walking man, as he looked straight into the face of this Rabbi, whose Name she heard the woman beside her say - "Yeshua."

The very moment she heard His Name spoken, He turned to Rivkah and held out to her a beautiful object in His hand and beckoned her to take it. Her body sprang forth with such abandonment as she reached out and received the tear bottle that was in her dream. She had met the Messiah through her tears of joy.

Thoughts To Meditate On:

As I would spend time studying and learning the Jewish roots of my faith, vivid scenes would spring forth from the ancient language. Scriptures came alive as I touched the roots of the olive tree and received the sap that flowed into my heart. And, suddenly, everything around me came alive as I read the Ancient Book, the Holy Bible.

In Psalm 56, there is a beautiful verse that ministered truth to me as I researched the scriptures to find out where I belong as a wild olive branch, and also to find out if the God of Israel loves me and has a plan for me beside His people Israel. I knew that many would miss the beauty of God's love to us now in this hour as they skimmed over scripture as if it were a daily cup of tea.

There is a story that is told about a tear bottle. When the soldiers of King David's time went to war, they would hand their loved ones a tear bottle. Those who were left to tend the home fires would cry their tears into this bottle while the soldier was off to war. When the warrior returned, he would immediately search out the tear bottle, hoping to find it full. This would tell him that he was loved and missed. He cherished that bottle with everything that was in him. Every teardrop was precious in his sight. He knew that each tear in the bottle was unique. One tear could be for the loneliness felt while he was gone, or for something sorrowful that happened while he was away. He knew how precious those tears were that were saved for him to see, but he also knew how priceless those tears were to the one who shed them. It was his greatest reward for the battles he fought. And it was also rewarding for the one who shed the tears, knowing that the beholder would cherish each one that had dropped into the bottle as the grief and sorrow had overtaken her in life's loneliness. To each it was a treasure of love that held the most intimate desire to be held by another and to not be questioned by the one who loves you and the one that you love.

That is the love affair the God of Israel has for His people. He has not changed His vows of everlasting love for her. Every tear that she sheds, He holds in His precious bottle that sits in His throne room, and those tears are also recorded on a scroll. "Those who sow in tears will reap with songs of joy" is a scripture of the Songs of Ascent in Psalm 126:5. This verse was read by the Jewish nation of Israel as they ascended to the Mountain of the Lord in Jerusalem, bearing their gifts of sacrifice to the Lord. It was the Jewish tears that flowed before ours were even formed. They watered the land of Israel to produce and bring forth the almond trees, the fig trees, and the pomegranate trees that will usher in the wedding scene that is to come on the Mount of Olives.

Every tear that has come from a Jewish soul has produced a wellspring, watering the desert which has become a garden of delight for you and I who have come into this garden. The Jewish tears have cost the heart of Israel many sorrowful nights, and now it is our time to give back and comfort them in this hour.

Scriptures To Know And Store In Our Hearts:

Psalm 56:8 "Record my lament; list my tears on your scroll – are they not in your record?" In another translation it says, "You number my wanderings; Put my tears into Your bottle; Are they not in Your book?" NKJV

Psalm 126:5 "Those who sow in tears will reap with songs of joy."

Isaiah 25:7-8 "On this mountain he will destroy the shroud that enfolds all peoples, the sheet that covers all nations; he will swallow up death forever. The Sovereign LORD will wipe away the tears from all faces; he will remove the disgrace of his people from all the earth. The

LORD has spoken."

Jeremiah 31:16 "This is what the LORD says: 'Restrain your voice from weeping and your eyes from tears, for your work will be rewarded,' declares the LORD. 'They will return from the land of the enemy.'"

Jeremiah 50:4-5 "'In those days, at that time,' declares the LORD, 'the people of Israel and the people of Judah together will go in tears to seek the LORD their God. They will ask the way to Zion and turn their faces toward it. They will come and bind themselves to the LORD in an everlasting covenant that will not be forgotten.'"

Luke 7:38 "... and as she stood behind him at his feet weeping, she began to wet his feet with her tears. Then she wiped them with her hair, kissed them and poured perfume on them."

Revelation 7:17 "For the Lamb at the center of the throne will be their shepherd; he will lead them to springs of living water. And God will wipe away every tear from their eyes."

Prayer of Revelation:

Abba, Father, in heaven,

Thank You for Your love for me and for Your desire to be close to me. I give You my tears, and I know You will watch over them and care for them and rain them down on the parched ground of others' lives. I know when my tears mingle with Your tears, we become inseparable. Your compassion becomes my compassion. Your love becomes my love for others. Your tenderness becomes my tenderness toward others. Thank You, Abba, for letting me release my tears before You and for not turning away during the times of my soul's wanderings. Thank You that You keep watch over them as they are recorded in my life's book. Thank You that every page, whether it is a page of laughter or a page of tears, is precious in Your eyes. Give me compassion, Holy Spirit, for the tears of my Jewish family as they have wept over their loss of lives. Let my tears mingle with Your people's tears that I may have a covenant of tears with them.

I ask this in HaShem, The Name that is above all names, Yeshua, Amen.

Yasmin – The Woven Garment of The Desert

She wondered why her garment was to be woven with the story that everyone else had determined would be her life. She had not even lived her story yet to have a woven garment made for man to read. They handed her the colored yarns that their minds saw for her, and she flinched as her eyes were assaulted by the harshness of brilliant orange and sunburst yellow flashing before her. Did they not know that her soul reached out for the deep blue of the sea waters, the green of a turning leaf before the winter snow overtook its life, or even the softness of scarlet that would wash over her as a precious sacrifice that, as yet, she knew not of?

It was her life's journey that was to be woven into the garment that would adorn her lovely, curved body still in its youthfulness. They told her that they had discussed her garment with the elders in the village and this is what had been decided for her life. She would "live" out the story woven into her garment before the villagers, and there would be no surprises to anyone because they just had to look at her garment to see what came next. Yasmin shuddered with resentment over the fact that others had control of her young life, and she felt like a betrayer of the leaders who were to pattern her life for the sake of the village and for the sake of tradition.

She had so much in her heart that she dreamed of outside the unseen village border that loomed large around her, circling her and watching her every day of her life. She wanted to walk with boldness over the invisible line that kept her inside this desert enclosure. She knew from her two travels to the next village that the desert had no end, yet she yearned to go as far as she could. She loved her people and wanted to be thankful for all that she had been provided with – food, clothing, warm tent at night, laughter and whispers of women telling stories as their fingers hid the movement of their lips from the elders of the village. But she cried in her heart, hoping that some unobservable force would come and sweep her onto an Arabian horse and take her into the desert night to begin to live in the freedom that rang in her heart.

She was mad in her mind as she silently voiced her desire, knowing that if the elders heard her say such things she would be severely disciplined and all the village would know she did not have the same heart as they had. Why did she have this ache in her heart? Why did she have the same dream all the time of someone weaving her a garment – though the hand that she saw was not the hand of a woman, but the hand of a man with strength in his fingers, yet possessing a gentleness that she knew would not harm her? She began to question her dream. How could a man be a weaver? Was she designing her own garment, or was it actually the strong, gentle hand of a man that she saw designing it? She did not care because she felt contented in the dream, knowing that the design in her garment was perfect and be beyond her wildest imaginations and desires.

Yasmin lay back on her mat and took into view the goat-haired tent that she helped weave with her mother and the other women of the village. Oh, she was well aware that the special weave shielded the harsh rays of the sun in the summer months and then mysteriously became tight in the winter months to keep out the cold and secure the warmth inside for the family. But all she could see was a black covering that held her enclosed in its lifeless form. "No!" she screamed in her heart, "This is not what the Unseen Designer has for me." Who is this One that she now so often called the "Unseen Designer"? She longed for the One that she somehow knew had a special design for her life-garment, just as the Creator had specially designed the desert around her.

Yasmin prepared for another journey to the next village where her father went to purchase the best goats the desert could offer. She loved this trip, but understood her father was pushing the rules of their way of life to the very edge by taking his daughter on a trip such as this. But he was able to tactfully make an excuse about why he needed her on this trip. She knew that her father's heart had ached for sons all these years, but her mother had only one seed that brought forth life in the early years, and that was Yasmin. Her father had been told he could bring in another wife to produce sons for him, but he could not even think about hurting the dear wife of his youth, no matter what their customs allowed. He was even brought before the village council, who encouraged him to act upon it immediately, but again, her father had a way with words and convinced the elders it was not in his best interest to do this.

She loved her father and admired his love for her mother. Her parents did not speak many verbal words between them, but their eyes spoke a thousand words to each other every time they met. Yasmin believed that every unspoken word of love between them had been recorded, and that she would someday discover a hidden scroll in the desert and read their love story. She was such a dreamer, but she cherished the dreams that she held in her heart. Too often, in the night hours, she would hear through her window the quarrels of the neighbor's many wives, and she resolved that she would never live like that. Yasmin escaped into her dream of finding her one, true love and speaking a thousand words to him with her eyes.

Yasmin heard her father's voice, Hadar, calling her to hurry up, that it was time to leave on their journey. She was eager because the journey required them to spend a night under the desert moon, both ways. She did not mind the cold nights because of the warm coverings her mother had lovingly made for her. The first day of travel was long and hot, but she relished every moment as she drank in the beauty of the landscape. Yasmin wore a gauzy veil to shield her face as much as she could from the burning rays of the sun, and she also applied layers of olive oil onto her silken skin to protect it. Even so, her skin was becoming darker with each passing day. It was inevitable in desert life. But she was determined not to look old and wrinkled at an early age like the other women in her camp, so she always carried a vessel of oil olive in a pouch under her garment.

Hadar had always given his daughter the best, and she was thankful for everything her father gave her. She was the light of his life, and she knew there was no one else like him. As a father, he possessed a certain understanding and love for her that she did not see in other fathers around her. He was a gift to her, just as the desert was a gift to her people. There was not one thing that any of them took for granted, nor did she. There was only one difference. They had their god, but Yasmin knew in her heart it was not the One who would be hers. She guarded these feelings, though, as she knew she would become a heartbreak to her family if they ever unearthed the thoughts in her heart. There were customs, and then there was their religion, but it was so dead to Yasmin. She wanted more, and knew that the Designer of the desert had also designed her. Yasmin believed that somewhere beyond the desert was the One she was searching for.

At last, she removed her petite frame from the camel as every bone in her body cried with a silent ache, but there would be no words of complaint to her father. She stroked her legs and felt the blood again begin to flow through her veins. Yasmin felt a contentment wash over her that she could not explain. Something told her at that moment that she was going to meet her destiny on this journey. How silly, but yet how strong this thought was took root in her very core. What destiny? Her father and mother had told her that soon her future would arrive in their village, a young man from the neighboring village who would become her husband. Yasmin shivered, but not from the dampness that comes with the desert nights. It was a shiver that sent a fearful trembling through her entire body. Yasmin decided that these thoughts of her future would not be a thief in the desert to come and steal her lovely night under the brilliantly lit desert sky.

Her father had made a temporary dwelling for the night's

sleep, which was perfect for her. It was a four-sided enclosure, with no roof, so she could enjoy the stars that danced and twirled in the night sky. To Yasmin, the display spoke of the courtship of love, as one lonely star would find another, and as the two became one, they swallowed up even more of the darkness around them. She so often wondered where these thoughts of love came from and why they would surface in such an inexperienced heart. Did the Desert Designer weave these thoughts in her even as she was hidden in her mother's womb, and then at the season of the budding of her womanhood, release them to the surface to be captured and acted out in the now of time? Yasmin snuggled beneath her warm wool blanket and fell into a deep sleep, and then the dream began.

The morning brought its wonderment as Yasmin stood and stretched her young body beneath the wash of sunbeams caressing her with tender care. Oh, how she did enjoy the moments of time that were given to her with freedom from the enclosure of her village. She knew her father loved to share these precious moments of freedom with her because soon he would no longer be able to give her a door of escape through which she could express her desire for adventure. Soon her husband would have the say in all that she would think and do. That is the way of their life and the traditions that are set for the women of their village.

She cast the encroaching thoughts of her future aside again as she embraced the day ahead. Today, their destination was Beersheba to barter with the goat breeder for an increase of her father's flock. She loved the activity of the town and the people busy with their lives' ventures. The goat breeder lived outside the town, but had many connections with other goat breeders that passed along this route. Climbing onto her four-legged beast, Yasmin settled into the hard, worn seat and wondered how many miles her mother had traveled upon the same seat.

She often thought of the cycles of life as she felt the changing of the seasons. The springtime had arrived with the buds of the fig tree bursting in anticipation of the abundance of the fruit yet to appear. Her mind began to remember the dream of the Desert Designer who had lovingly touched her garment and had opened her eyes to the colors of her desires. Yes, they were there in the memory of last night's dream – images of blues, greens and deep scarlet that captivated her soul. The gentle, strong hands that seemed to say to her, "I will protect and shield you behind My shelter of love, and there you will live to love Me and I will love you." Just then, as though he knew she was lost in her daydream, the four-legged creature stumbled, jarring her attention to the fact that they were coming into Beersheba.

Her father was good at his trade as a goatherd and he had earned the respect of those who had witnessed his good heart and also his shrewdness. The purchasing and trading was finished before the last ray of the sun kissed Yasmin's cheeks. She lingered in the warmth of the sun's kiss that stirred a yearning to be kissed with tenderness by the One who would cover her with His name.

Entering one more time the four-sided enclosure built by her loving father's hand for his daughter's sacred privacy, she was once again thankful for the open heaven to be able to dream her dreams of the Desert Designer. If only the stars could speak and tell a story of the romances and the wild fantasy of a young maiden's heart, or dare to speak of the prince who rides through the desert sand to be enraptured by the princess who takes his breath away. She wondered if, one day, when everything fades away and the earth becomes void, would the words of two lovers' passion for one another repaint its surface? Is there a place where the Bridegroom is altogether perfect and His bride shines with a light that radiates through her veil in devotion to the One who stands alongside her, attending to the needs of her heart?

Yasmin decided that the stars did hold that story and were speaking it to the inhabitants of the desert, but their ears were not yet opened to hear of this magnificent love story. She wondered why her own young ears could hear it while those around her seemed to only hear everyday words of survival in their older, supposedly more mature ears. She yearned to break free and be rescued from a predictable, ordinary life. Something told her that inside she already had, and that very soon she would touch the eternal realm of understanding her own heart and knowing the reason why she was brought forth for such a time as this in this desert place. Yasmin entered into the realm of the Desert Designer as she took the deep breaths that led her into His chamber.

With an excitement in her heart, she awoke yet again to a new beginning in her life's journey. Today they would enter the town of Sychar near Mt. Gerizim where her father would pick out a beaded necklace for his wife, to give to her on the day of remembrance of their desert wedding. He did not, however, allow the other elders of the village to know of his tenderness for his loving wife. He would be chided with disapproving looks and would sense their disdain of his romantic heart. Still, that would never stop him, for it was his wife who kept him happy in their secret place of coming together as one body. Not even their disapproving looks could make him turn away from the bride of his youth.

Yasmin was so excited and distracted by all that she saw that she started to slip sideways off the beast and managed to right herself just in the nick of time before the embarrassing thud could happen. A sudden thirst hit her and she knew her father would allow her to go to the well in the center of town. Even though it was not the proper time to go, her father would overlook that and give his heart away with a smile, knowing full well what was happening with his beautiful daughter. She adored him.

As they entered the town, she noticed women whispering under their veils as if they held the latest gossip of the hour. Sometimes it saddened her to see women try to soothe the pain in their hearts with something that brought even more pain – gossip. She had promised herself that she would never become like the women who sat and threw word-stones at another empty soul who was just yearning to have her heart filled with a reason to even exist. Yasmin believed that every person alive had a story of wanting something but not knowing what. Why some of them thought it was okay to hurl insults at another, she did not know. The only thing she could figure was that maybe they thought they could hide their own emptiness by looking down on someone else. Even the men of the village would stare at another's field and fine flocks and be filled with an emptiness because they felt they never had enough. But why should everyone feel so empty? Yasmin knew that the One who made it all wanted to give them even more, but most of all, He wanted to fill them on the inside of their vessels with an abundance that nature could not give, only He could. As He created the world around them with the beauty of nature, this One also wanted to fill their hearts with the beauty of His created love.

How does she know these things in her inward parts? How has she gone through this veil of understanding? Has it opened its way to her because of the willingness of her heart to know the unseen One who is wooing her? The Desert Designer has once again captured her thoughts. Who is He that she trusts Him with the secrets that are deep within the treasure chest of her heart? Somehow she knows He will not hurt or harm her as He makes His way into the hidden chamber of her desires. She instinctively feels safe in His presence, this One she has named the Desert Designer, who has woven her garment of desires that He has lovingly placed upon her but is unseen by others. Her father always would say with a chuckle, "What is it, Yasmin, that brings a smile to your face even while you are tending to your chores? Is there something that you want to tell your father that delights my daughter so?" She would try desperately to hold back the blush that would flood her body. She did not yet understand the depth of her father's words that would awaken her once again to the memory of her dreams of the One who fulfilled her and knew her deep passion to be loved on the inside of her vessel, knowing that it would extend to the outside of her vessel.

As she approached the well, she overheard a voice that dripped like honey and yet commanded such respect and authority that it took her breath away. She looked up and saw a most intriguing Man. He wore the garments of a Rabbi, but He was talking with a woman who she could plainly see was a woman of ill repute. The scene she was witnessing did not fit into her world of rules of conduct between a man and a woman, but yet it was unsoiled to her eyes of innocence. Yasmin knew she should not be listening to the words that flowed from this Jewish Rabbi's mouth, but even as one outside the Jewish community, she knew she was witnessing something that would change her life.

She was captivated by the look of tenderness in the Jewish man's eyes as He took the cup of water from her hands without touching her, except with His words. The woman seemed to want to run from Him. Yasmin thought it was because she was a Samaritan, who were considered by the Jews to be nothing more than dogs. The woman's garment was soiled and torn on one side, causing it to slip off her left shoulder as if to proclaim to the Stranger at the well, "She is unclean. Look, I will show you." The garment seemed to have its own voice that it desperately wanted the Jewish Stranger to hear and so turn away from the woman held captive by it, but the Stranger did not move from the well.

Yasmin began to hear the sound of flowing water, but the well nearby was silent in its depth. She put her fingers into her ears and shook her delicate head to try to stop the sound of the water coming to her. The sun was hot, and maybe there was an attack upon her mind that was affecting her hearing. But suddenly, there was a peace inside her that made her realize that was not the case. She again turned her attention to the well and knew that she was witnessing a transforming moment for the woman who was shrouded in the soiled garment. Suddenly she heard the gentle Rabbi say to her, "I who speak to you am he." She turned and, lifting her garment to reveal long, slender legs, seemed to run with the swiftness of a young gazelle. What had happened to this woman that brought a youthful strength and innocence to her worn out body that had been abused with shame and disgrace for so long?

Yasmin's heart began to pound with an excitement that she could not fully comprehend, but all of a sudden, the dream of the Desert Designer broke through the veil of her thoughts and she quaked with a delight that entered every part of her body and she heard her own words, "Is He the Desert Designer of my garment?"

She collapsed to the ground and did not even know how long she sat in silence until she heard a commotion. First, men's voices, and then the woman's voice, "There is the Man who told me everything I ever did. Look, He is the One standing at the well." Yasmin stood spellbound and could not believe what she was seeing. The woman at the well had a fresh, spotless woven garment draped upon her as though she had become royalty in a split second. Yasmin rubbed her eyes to see more clearly the new garment that spoke its words to the villagers, "I am a newly woven garment of beauty, woven by the Desert Designer, to be worn from this day forth."

Yasmin held her breath as she heard someone say, "He is the Rabbi from Nazareth that some say is the Son of God who will give you living water and weave you a garment of righteousness of His love to you." Yasmin knew she had met the Desert Designer as He turned and looked into her eyes and walked into her heart to live forever.

Thoughts To Meditate On:

How many of us have wanted new garments to wear upon our bodies that would make us feel good on the inside and look good on the outside. I have discovered that this desire is not only for women, but also for men – to feel good when they have on a smart, put-together outfit. The Lord has put this desire in each of us, but, really, it is the desire to wear His righteousness as a garment upon us.

Many of us, as non-Jews, do not have the depth of understanding of the importance of a garment in the Middle East. Even today, Bedouin women prize the woven garments that tell the story of their life's journey for all to read. In the western culture, those of us who read the Word of God forget that the Bible was written by our Jewish ancestors in the eastern culture setting. Truly, even as wild olive branches grafted into the "real-rooted olive tree," we are to adapt to the sap that flows from the tree and become like the natural branches, manifesting the same garment of leaves that brings forth healing for all nations.

When the apostle Paul was speaking to the non-Jewish believers in Rome, he gave such a visual picture of the garment we are to wear,

"Instead, clothe yourselves with the Lord Yeshua the Messiah." CJB He is saying to the Gentiles who have now converted to the ways of the Ancient Torah truths to wear the robe of salvation of the Messiah, Yeshua. Everything in Yeshua's garments speaks of His Jewish lineage and of His people, Israel. We cannot question that we are to be transported by the Spirit into the Jewish culture of our Lord Yeshua and to wear His garments of salvation.

Scriptures To Meditate On:

2 Chronicles 6:41 *"Now arise, O LORD God, and come to your resting place, you and the ark of your might. May your priests, O LORD God, be clothed with salvation, may your saints rejoice in your goodness."*

Psalm 45:13-14 *"All glorious is the princess within her chamber; her gown is interwoven with gold. In embroidered garments she is led to the king; her virgin companions follow her and are brought to you."*

Isaiah 52:1 *"Awake, awake, O Zion, clothe yourself with strength. Put on your garments of splendor, O Jerusalem, the holy city. The uncircumcised and defiled will not enter you again."*

Isaiah 61:10 *"I delight greatly in the LORD; my soul rejoices in my God. For he has clothed me with garments of salvation and arrayed me in a robe of righteousness, as a bridegroom adorns his head like a priest, and as a bride adorns herself with her jewels."*

Ezekiel 16:8 *"Later I passed by, and when I looked at you and saw that you were old enough for love, I spread the corner of my garment over you and covered your nakedness. I gave you my solemn oath and entered into a covenant with you, declares the Sovereign LORD, and you became mine."*

Zechariah 3:3-4 *"Now Joshua was dressed in filthy clothes as he stood before the angel. The angel said to those who were standing before him, 'Take off his filthy clothes.' Then he said to Joshua, 'See, I have taken away your sin, and I will put rich garments on you.'"*

Revelation 19:7-8 *"Let us rejoice and be glad and give him glory! For the wedding of the Lamb has come, and his bride has made herself ready. Fine linen, bright and clean, was given her to wear."*

Prayer of Revelation:

Dear Abba, Father,

How good You are to us the wild olive branches to teach us of Your ways. Forgive us that we have not acknowledged Your people and the insight that the Holy Spirit has wanted us to see and understand. Strip us of our religious garments and the set ways of our western culture and give us revelation of the significance of the garments that You have placed upon us to be read by all men. May Your Name, Yeshua, and Your Word be seen in the garments of righteousness that we are to wear with thankfulness. May all nations read Your life woven into the threads of our garments and say, "Take us to the mountain of the Lord. As you are going, we also will go."

In Yeshua's Name.

Amen.

Rebekah – A Sealed Spring

Her life had become so busy, but she knew it was because of her own choices. The busier she was, the less time she had to think about running away from everything she knew was proper. Rebekah caught herself again wondering what it would be like to live away from the busy city and to be known as a desert woman. She had never understood why she felt as though she did not fit into her own life. It was like she was a wild desert flower planted in a clay pot, struggling to keep alive without a drop of water. Rebekah waited patiently for a day to come when she would find herself somewhere other than where she was. How ungrateful she felt every time these thoughts entered her mind.

As she walked through the town, she was well aware that there were many who would love to have a life like hers. Like the woman of ill-repute that Rebekah always saw on a certain street corner. She always wore a scarlet scarf around her face, her piercing blue eyes peering out. Rebekah could sense the cry of help in her eyes each time she saw her. What could she do, as a single woman, to help when there were so many like the scarlet-clad woman? Day after day, they waited for the lonely traveler to come across their path.

In Rebekah's opinion, the man was the real marauder. But the community labeled only the women. The words used to describe them were so ugly that she couldn't bring herself to repeat them out loud. What if she were to find herself in a circumstance such as those young women in the alleyways, and ended up in the same state they were?

Rebekah's heart melted with compassion for them, and many times she gave them smiles as she passed by. But the one with the scarlet scarf always stood out to Rebekah because of her pleading eyes.

Each day they would give their bodies and souls away for a few shekels. The stranger would come, his life concealed, not to be questioned by anyone. But the woman on the street was known by all. It did not seem the least bit fair to Rebekah that the one who was being used to satisfy another person's desperate need for flesh was the one every finger pointed at – the woman, and not the man.

It was the man who should be known as the person of ill-repute because of his shameless desire to use another human body that did not belong to him to give him a release. Was it alright for a man to take another when he had a wife waiting for him at home as he journeyed throughout the land, or had a fiancée counting the days until they would become one? Rebekah did not think so.

It did not matter to the society; the woman was always at fault, period. Why wasn't the man ever stoned? Why was the woman always stoned? Rebekah could not reconcile this injustice in her mind, no matter how she looked at it. To most people, these women did not have names or faces, but to Rebekah they all had faces and names. Her heart wanted to reach out and let them know that, but how? So far, her many questions went unanswered. She did know one thing, however: that the same God who created her created these women, too. And she knew that each of these women desired a husband to love them and have a family, just as she desired it. But sometimes Rebekah had to try to banish all of these concerns from her mind and just give to them what she could, and that was compassion with a smile.

Today she was to meet a woman merchant from the village of Sychar in Samaria. If others knew what she was doing, their advice to Rebekah would be, "Do not go to meet this woman. But if you must do business with her, send a man – not from any of the tribes of Israel, but a foreigner."

Rebekah was purchasing a special ointment that was known to cure the sting from an obnoxious plant which seemed innocent enough until you happened to walk into its path and meet its wrath. This plant did not have any discrimination when it came to victims – young, old, man, woman, child. The pain was intense and lasted for a lengthy time, but if you applied this special ointment, it would disappear within minutes.

The women in Samaria knew of a secret ingredient to combine with other well-known ones in an olive oil base. The secret ingredient was never divulged to anyone outside their village, which Rebekah understood was for their own reasons, rights, and financial gain. All the women in the village benefited from it whether single, widowed, or married.

She had sympathy for the people of Samaria who were sent to Israel by the King of Assyria and were known to the Jews as dogs. Their territory was between Judea and the Galilee and was connected by a road that Jews would not take. They always went the longer way around to the Galilee. Rebekah knew that the Samaritans worshiped the God of Israel on Mt. Gerizim and not on Mt. Moriah in Jerusalem. Besides all the whispers she'd heard from other Jewish women, she knew that these people were greatly discriminated against. She was not interested in looking for the differences between her women and the women of Samaria; she tried to look at the similarities, woman to woman, with the same basic needs in life.

At the meeting point, Rebekah saw a woman standing with her head down, holding a small bundle in her hand. This had to be the merchant woman who had come all the way from Samaria to sell her cure for the sting of the nasty weed that always managed to find Rebekah or a friend of hers. Finally, the woman looked up, revealing the most beautiful smile Rebekah had ever seen, with the whitest teeth that glistened as the sun shone on them.

The beauty of this woman took Rebekah by surprise, and she was ashamed when she realized that deep down, she had been prejudiced and actually was expecting the woman to be different or even be one that her people would call a dog. She asked forgiveness in the quietness of her heart and thanked the Lord for this opportunity to meet another woman like herself living in this beautiful land of abundance. Rebekah reaffirmed her belief that it didn't matter where each woman came from; they were a woman first before anything else.

The lovely woman came forward and introduced herself as Shayna, greeting her with another smile. Instantly, Rebekah wanted to respond with a friendly kiss on each cheek, but refrained in case it might offend her in some way.

Rebekah thanked Shayna for coming all the way to the outskirts of Jerusalem so she could purchase the special ointment, and hoped that they could arrange to meet at this spot every six months or so. She wanted Shayna to feel comfortable so she went on and on about how much she liked her ointment and that maybe she could help find more people to sell it to. As she was talking, Rebekah sensed something in her – like she was excited but was trying to maintain composure. So she asked Shayna about her excitement – was she happy about meeting face to face? Was she happy at the prospect of having more customers? Or was there another reason for the excitement within her? Shayna blurted out that her whole village was in an uproar because a woman of ill-repute had been going through the whole town telling everyone that she had met the Messiah. Shayna said she was happy for the woman because she really had been transformed and was no longer one who took men into bed with her. She also mentioned to her that she heard that this Rabbi was on His way to Jerusalem, so she had been looking to see if she might meet him on the road.

Rebekah knew at once that Shayna must come with her to Jerusalem to tell the young woman with the scarlet scarf this wonderful story of deliverance and maybe she could be set free, too. When Rebekah asked her, Shayna replied with enthusiasm that it would be her delight to come and see a woman be set free from the pains of yesterday. Shayna told her that if she could stay overnight at Rebekah's, even though she knew it was forbidden for a Jew to even touch her, she would be willing to come, but that it was up to Rebekah. Shayna couldn't believe she said such a bold thing, knowing that it would put Rebekah at risk.

Rebekah did not hesitate. She knew deep inside that it was not the rules of the Rabbis dictating her decision; it was her heart that had already chosen life for someone else. The two women embraced each other with the hope that maybe one day this unknown woman of ill-repute would also be in their embrace. Rebekah led the way into the city after wrapping her shawl around Shayna's shoulders, believing that if her neighbors saw her shawl on Shayna's shoulders, they would think that she must be a distant relative that had come to spend the night with Rebekah. In her heart she prayed, "Let it be your will, God of Abraham, Isaac and Jacob."

On their way through the city, Rebekah chose a path that she knew would lead to the woman with the scarlet scarf. She believed that God would fill their mouths with something to say to her. But would the woman even acknowledge them, or would she shun them as she had been shunned by the neighborhood women? They had to try. Before them in the distance was the woman, and Rebekah prayed again, "Dear God, please may this Rabbi be the Messiah that has come to set my people Israel free, as well as others who call on His Name, and may this one that we are about to speak to respond in acceptance to our words and not turn in fear."

Slowly they walked up, allowing the woman time to see them. The young woman kept her eyes on both of them and was motionless. She looked as if she was a statue that had fallen but had not yet crumbled. Rebekah took a deep breath and said, "May we talk with you for just a moment?" The sweetest sound came forth out of this unnamed woman's mouth that it startled Rebekah as she realized how young she really was. The response that came to her was, "As you please."

Rebekah started by retelling Shayna's story and pleading with this young woman to come with both of them to the temple steps because they had heard of a Rabbi who set a woman in Sychar free from this way of life and they think He might be here in

Jerusalem and maybe He could do the same for her. Rebekah's words gushed like a river and then she abruptly stopped, staring into the young girl's blue eyes, waiting for a response. It seemed like an eternity passed and they hoped they had not frightened her with their eagerness. Finally, they heard a faint whisper, "I will come." Rebekah breathed a sigh of relief and looked down to see that Shayna was kneeling beside the trembling young girl, holding her hand.

Tears sprang up in Rebekah as though she had been a sealed up spring of water that had just been loosed. As they stood together, Rebekah realized that they must first stop at her house for this young girl to put on other garments to at least cover the outward appearance of her life's circumstance. Rebekah would have given her every one of her robes, she was so happy inside, and yet they had not even met the mysterious Rabbi who set a woman free from bondage.

Quietly, without any talking, they slipped into Rebekah's little house and changed her clothes. Suddenly Shayna said, "What is your name?" realizing they had not even asked her! Out of this little one's body came the name, "Yehudit." At that moment, she became a real person, with a real name and a real story of her life's struggle. They were all moved, and their tears joined as one.

They left Rebekah's house and made their way to the temple, praying to be seen as ordinary women longing to worship and bring their offerings. Yet Rebekah knew that inside they were all trembling with hope and praying that no one would be disappointed in this One who caused all of Sychar to take notice.

In their excitement, their steps had quickened and they were all talking at once when they suddenly came upon a crowd of religious men shouting accusations against a woman who lay on the ground as if she was dead. The three looked at the woman as they walked around the crowd and they saw her tears falling with such great sorrow that a puddle had formed beneath her face. Dust would spring up, leaving muddied streaks across her face, and the horrible sight brought the trio to a halt. How could this be happening right before them? What would happen to this woman? Rebekah felt Yehudit shudder, and she quickly wrapped her arm around her to hold her steady, as did Shayna. They were bound together, three cords securely wrapped in love for each other, and nothing was going to separate their longing to see each other's hunger met and for each other to be free from the inside out.

The scribes and the Pharisees were gathered like vultures, ready to tear this woman apart, each smug face looking as though it had been applauded by God Himself for bringing this woman forward. Rebekah looked on with astonishment and tugged on Shayna's sleeve and said, "Is He the One that was in Sychar?" Shayna looked up and with delight said, "Yes, He must be the One, look at His face. There is no face as kind as that in all the earth."

The next thing they heard was the crowd of men saying to the Rabbi, "Teacher, this woman was caught in adultery, in the very act." Rebekah held Yehudit's hand tightly as the atmosphere grew in hostility. The lack of sympathy for the woman lying on the ground was as bold as a lion coming out for its kill. The religious men had circled her and formed an immovable wall of enclosure, where not even the sleekest prey could find its freedom. The women then heard someone say the words "Stone her," and each of them wanted to scream at the top of their lungs, "Enough!"

How did these men find this woman in the act of sexual intercourse, anyway? Were they all peering into the house and watching with their own eyes? Was not their own flesh aroused? These thoughts were in Rebekah's mind as she was again coming to the conclusion, "Who was really guilty in this hideous scene?" The men of religious standing who knew the Bible, yet also added their own ways of judgment on each person, or the poor woman who ended up without a relative to take responsibility for her and give her covering? Instinctively, Rebekah understood that this woman, like herself, Shayna, and Yehudit, was a closed up spring with no way to release the waters inside to flow out freely.

Without a word, the Rabbi stooped down and began to write something in the dirt. This silent response to the accusations baffled everyone, but it didn't stop their barrage against the woman. Words again poured like a flood from the religious men's mouths. The Rabbi stood and without a raised voice said to them, "If any one of you is without sin, let him be the first to throw a stone at her." It seemed that even the noisy temple court became silent as the words of love and life for the woman flowed out to everyone who had ears to hear. Yehudit began to cry, then Shayna's whimpering gasp was heard, and Rebekah felt her whole insides turn about as if everything in her was being rearranged by someone's hand. Her heart flooded with love for this Rabbi.

One by one, the religious men, beginning with the oldest, reluctantly walked away, their hearts still eager to see their hatred met. Even the youngest among them realized that the endeavor had failed and that their status as religious men, who welcomed the fear and reverence of the community, had evaporated before them.

When the dust had settled, the Rabbi turned to the woman and with such clarity and calmness said to her, "Woman, where are they? Has no one condemned you?" She said, "No one, sir." And then with such authority, He said, "Then neither do I condemn you. Go now and leave your life of sin. I am the light of the world. Whoever follows me will never walk in darkness, but will have the light of life."

Rebekah and her two friends ran to the woman and fell down and wrapped their arms around her and wept with happiness for her and for each other. Inside each of them, waters were being released to be loved and to give love. Their sealed springs had come alive with surging waters of happiness and joy. Rebekah looked up and met the eyes of this mysterious Rabbi and knew who He really was.

Thoughts To Meditate On:

How can we, as women of the Bible, condemn another to death when we had death in our own lives before we met the "Real Rabbi" sent by the Father Himself? Have we become callous to one another and impenetrable to the loving forgiveness that God offers each one of us through His Son the Rabbi?

As we look at the story of these three women, Rebekah, Shayna and Yehudit, they become a measuring rod as to how we are with each other, and especially as to how we look at others who are not as fortunate as we are to know that there is One who paid the price for all our sins on the execution stake. God's love transcends every race, color, and even nation of people who will receive His love and forgiveness for them.

Women who have not come to acknowledge Him are like an open spring for all to come and drink from, but the ones who know Him know that only the man that God has destined for them as their husband can drink of these sweet waters.

In Song of Songs 4:12, "You are a garden locked up, my sister, my bride; you are a spring enclosed, a sealed fountain." In this scripture King Solomon is describing his virgin love that has not been opened yet to receive love and to give love. Another way to look at this scripture is that the garden represents the Garden of Eden that is closed off to the ways of the world. "They are not of the world, just as I am not of the world." NKJV . John 17:16 says it all. We women of God have been set apart for His glory to manifest His love to all who call on the Rabbi's Name, Yeshua.

Natural sealed springs are found in the land of Israel, and, of course, the inspired, anointed scribes who wrote down the words of the Bible knew all about them and understood what they were. But those in the church who live in places other than the land of Israel have a hard time understanding the deep meaning of this scripture. So let's go even deeper as women who have been created by God to be joined as one with the husband that will be. Just as the bride of Christ is a virgin, as new believers we also become virgins, as though we have never been touched by any defiling act or hand of the flesh. We become a sealed spring unto Him. When we receive Him into our hearts and He lives in us, the waters begin to flow for the whole world to see and exclaim, "This one is no longer parched ground, but a well-watered garden of delight."

The sweet women in the story all longed to be set free by God's love, and they found their Bondage-Breaker in the true Living Waters of delight, the Jewish Messiah, who now had become all three women's Redeemer.

Another scripture that also describes what Yeshua did against the enemies of our souls is found in 1 Chronicles 14:11 "So they went up to Baal Perazim, and David defeated them there. Then David said, 'God has broken through my enemies by my hand like a breakthrough of water.' Therefore they called the name of that place Baal Perazim." NKJV

The Lord Himself has risen up like many waters and has washed our spots, our wrinkles, and our blemishes away in the flesh. Though one was Jewish, one a Samaritan, and one of ill-repute, the Rabbi came for all of them just like He came for all of us, whether we are Jewish, non-Jewish, or of ill-repute.

In this story, Rebekah, Shayna and Yehudit found freedom. So can you!

Scriptures To Know And Store In Our Hearts:

<u>Genesis 2:10</u> "Now a river went out of Eden to water the garden, and from there it parted and became four riverheads." NKJV

<u>Jeremiah 31:12</u> "Therefore they shall come and sing in the height of Zion, streaming to the goodness of the LORD—For wheat and new wine and oil, for the young of the flock and the herd; their souls shall be like a well-watered garden, And they shall sorrow no more at all." NKJV

<u>Jeremiah 17:13</u> "O LORD, the hope of Israel, all who forsake You shall be ashamed. 'Those who depart from Me shall be written in the earth, because they have forsaken the LORD, the fountain of living waters.'" NKJV (author's note: this scripture describes the action of Yeshua as he wrote in the ground while the Pharisees and scribes were looking on.)

<u>Ecclesiastes 2:5-6</u> "I made myself gardens and orchards, and I planted all kinds of fruit trees in them. I made myself water pools from

which to water the growing trees of the grove." NKJV

Ephesians 5:27 "... that He might present her to Himself a glorious church, not having spot or wrinkle or any such thing, but that she should be holy and without blemish." NKJV

Revelation 21:27 "But there shall by no means enter it anything that defiles, or causes an abomination or a lie, but only those who are written in the Lamb's Book of Life." NKJV

Prayer of Revelation:

Dear Abba, Father,

We come with our hearts fully before You – not hiding ourselves behind a tree in the Garden as we hear You walking. We run to You and confess our weaknesses and fears of not understanding Your love to all people, especially to Your people Israel, and ask Your forgiveness. I ask that my parched soul would become a well-watered garden so others will see what receiving Your love and forgiveness can do for a woman without any hope. Let me be a sign of hope to women of all the nations.

Amen.

Shoshana – Winter Is Past, Spring Has Come

Shoshana eagerly awaited the first sign of spring to come to the land, her ears beckoning the turtledoves to begin their serenade in the fields around her habitation. It had been a cold winter. Every morning, she would wrap her large shawl around her slight frame and begin the morning's journey. No matter how sharp the wind was during this season, she never missed the daily outing to the market and to the Temple to pray.

She steeled herself for the brisk walk and opened the door. Something felt different today. The air even smelled different. She breathed in deeply and marveled at how quickly, after such a long winter season, things could change. She even heard the song of the turtledove for the first time. The sound of that lovely bird awakened her senses to the hour of her people, Israel. Would this be the season that the Messiah would come? Would He come and make Himself known to those in the Temple courts? Would He come to a lowly peasant girl from Jericho? Somehow, she knew in her heart that the Messiah her people longed for would consider even the lowliest of handmaidens in the land. No one had told her that, she just believed in her own heart that is the way the Messiah would be.

Shoshana opened her eyes to see the emerging blossoms on the trees. She felt the hardships of the winter months begin to fade away and the warmth of spring begin to enter her bones. Winter to Shoshana was a time of exile, a time of the full awareness of what her people went through in Egypt. How the hardship of slavery was always there in their memory. It didn't matter if hundreds of years had passed; it was as though it had happened yesterday. Every Pesach, her people would remember the exodus into freedom. Every Pesach, her people would remember the bitterness of those days. But every Pesach, her people would remember that Yahweh sent a deliverer named Moses to deliver them from Pharaoh and their bondage.

So to Shoshana, early spring was the time to remember that only Yahweh could bring His people out of exile and into the promised land where she now lived. She sensed that the rain in the last few months was somehow cleansing the land for an arrival, but of who or what, she did not know. She could smell the grapevines coming alive and see the first signs of the almond tree begin to emerge with purity and undefiled beauty. The song of the turtledoves was to her like the songs of the priests in the Temple raising their voices to welcome the Shekinah glory of Yahweh. Everything was coming alive, and it was a reminder to her people that the Great I Am was still amongst them and was reminding them of His Presence and His faithfulness.

Every spring, Shoshana brought out the dried flower seeds she had gathered in the fall and scattered them along the path that led to her little home. The time for sowing and giving back to the earth to again replenish it with life seeds was here again in the land. The soft cushion of earth seemed to drink in and welcome the intrusion of the seed-treasures into its private chambers. It was as if the whole land of Israel was sending out an invitation for someone or something to take part in the great mystery of sowing and reaping, the result of which was always to the benefit of the inhabitants dwelling on the earth's surface.

Awareness was heightened in this season, and she felt that the land itself was thirsty for the Messiah, just as her people were. It seemed to hold a secret, but could not release it to the people until the season was at hand. It was much like the way every soon-to-be-mother somehow senses that her unborn child knows the exact time to come forth for the outside world to see, no longer to be hidden within the secret enclosure of the womb.

So also, Shoshana knew to be aware of the season that had come upon her people and to stay alert in this hour for the prophets' words to come to pass. Her people still murmured and complained about the delay of the Messiah. Where was He? It reminded her of her people in the wilderness. She chose to keep her hope alive with seeds from the Torah Scroll. She embraced the seeds of truth when she heard the men talking in the courts of Solomon's colonnades. She listened with earnestness to every word, and ate them as she would a sweet morsel of Challah bread. She rehearsed by heart the words of the Prophet Isaiah, "And the Redeemer will come to Zion." Is this why the turtledoves are singing with exuberance and the blossoms are releasing their fragrance over the land? She felt the land was laying out a welcome mat for the One that is to come. She would be ready to wave her palm branches high to the heavens to welcome Him who is the Messiah of her people Israel.

She ascended the steps to the Temple Courts to bring an offering of thankfulness for her family before the crowds of Passover pilgrims flowed into Jerusalem two weeks from now. It always reminded her of a reverse river, defying the laws of gravity and flowing uphill instead of down. How good her Heavenly Father was to reveal His love and draw His people to Himself.

Her earthly father also had a way of revealing his heart of love to his family. Shoshana believed it was because his love for the God of Israel was as real to him as his love for his wife and children. Shoshana desired that quality in the man who would one day be her husband. Love was the center of all things to every Israelite marriage. Her people were not ashamed of the passion in marriage and the holiness of a man and a woman coming together as one. She knew that her father and mother melted into each other as the cycle for her mother to exhibit her womanhood to her father came twice a month. And as a young woman, soon to be matched to a young man in her village, Shoshana had been taught the importance of understanding the cycles and seasons of changes in her body. As a woman began her menstrual time, she was to stay clear of her husband because it was the time for the unclean blood and debris to flow out of her womb.

After seven days, the woman went to the mikveh to complete the cleansing of her secret chambers with fresh, living water. Yahweh provided a season of cleansing and He had also given the woman He made a season of rest from giving to another. After the oil, lotion, and preparation of her body on the next Shabbat night, she was ready for the life of her husband to enter her temple, knowing she was clean for his arrival. The anticipation was at its highest for the husband and the wife. Waiting in the outer courts was a picture for both of them – that after they had brought their sacrifice, they could then enter into a more intimate time with the Lord – so it was with each other. How beautiful!

Shoshana grieved for young women of pagan, roman ways who did not know of the beauty of lovemaking and the reward of a holy awareness of God's approval over the marriage bed. For just as he created Adam and Eve to enjoy each other in intimacy, His plan has not changed for His people Israel to this very day. Often, she would see the look of satisfaction on her parents' faces when they had awakened to the morning light after the evening of Shabbat. Her mother had a glow on her face, and her father had a contentment that always permeated the atmosphere of their home. Did Shoshana feel uncomfortable with knowing that the secret place of her body would be entered into by the man who would be her husband? The answer was yes, but the changes in her body were telling her she was ready to know and to feel this mystery between her soon-to-be husband and herself.

As her body went through seasons of change related to the cycle of the moon, so her people, Israel, were set on the cycle of the moon, also. The Lord never surprised them with unexpected events. The feasts that were set as everlasting ordinances always brought peace to her people. The seasons of the harvest and the fruit that spoke of the Lord's faithfulness to her people were always reminders that He was, is, and always will be faithful to let her people know the season they are in and the season of the coming of the Messiah.

She remembered the Torah portion that spoke to the children of Israel about the abundance of fruit that was given to them in their purposed seasons, selected by the hand of the Lord in the beginning of time. He was always reminding them that He set the seasons to reveal who He is. He set the feast of His coming and His presence amongst them. He informed Israel that He was bringing them into a land of wheat, barley, vines, fig trees, pomegranates, olive oil and honey. Each had its own season. And together they brought forth the abundance of His promised provision. Her people would not lack nor be without if they followed and honored His ways and His timing for all things.

Shoshana often reflected upon the abundance of good things the Lord had given her people. She loved the pomegranate with its beautiful red inhabitants beneath its hard covering. In the late summer months, her mother always had a bowl of pomegranates in the center of her table. Even the priests' garments were adorned with this fruit on the hem of their robes. Because she was a romantic young woman waiting for the love of her life, she was reminded of a saying she had heard from the women of her village. They would whisper that the season of the pomegranate was upon a young woman about to enter the chuppah of marriage. She had asked her mother what they meant, and her mother explained to her that the handmaiden in the book of Solomon had pronounced to her lover that because the pomegranates were in bloom, she would now give her love to him. It always brought a flush to her skin as she recalled the words of the handmaiden, a woman in love who knew the season to give her body in total abandonment and total assurance that it was God's time for her and the bridegroom to come together.

The fig tree was also a symbol to her people. Just as the leaves hide the fruit from sight and it takes someone to search for the hidden treasures of sweetness, so it is for a man to search for the woman who will bring sweetness into his life.

The date palm blossoms with enormous leaves sheltering a

cluster of fruit. The rich, dark honey it yields is beyond compare. When it ripens, all of Israel reaches upward to receive its abundance with gladness. In its season, it gives more than the eye can behold, just as a woman in her season gives an abundance of sweetness from her soul to her husband-to-be.

The wheat comes in its perfect season, too. As the first rains fall from the heavens to the earth, the seeds begin to germinate and then the latter rains soak the kernels, bringing the wheat to its ripened stage, filled with its rich source of life. This was all in the season of Passover. Shoshana also overheard the women in her village say that the wheat head represents the woman's womb after she has been watered by her husband in the early season of marriage, and as a result, is filled with life ready to be harvested.

The barley harvest arrived right on time, fifty days after Passover when the celebration of the Feast of Shavuot was at its peak. This was the season of the Lord for Ruth and Boaz. Only on the threshing floor could Ruth let Boaz know of her intentions as she lay at his feet. The joy of wine, the smell of barley, the reminder of the Torah given to her people at Mt. Sinai were confirmation to Shoshana once again that the Lord is on time for His people and that He has given them the enjoyment of rehearsing what is to come.

Olive oil was one of the most precious and versatile treasures to her people Israel. Harvest time followed the hot growing season of the olives, and another joyous celebration of thanksgiving for the abundance ensued. This amazing oil was used to light not only the great menorah in the Temple, but also the humble lamps in every home in Israel. It kept their women's skin like silk and was also used to clean their dwellings. From the highest use to the most mundane, God once again provided for every need of His people.

The wine that flowed from the sloping hills of their land was Israel's greatest symbol of rejoicing with gladness. Shoshana's favorite celebrations had to be the weddings, with the hosts providing brimming vats of the finest wines. These celebrations were joyous rehearsals of the much-anticipated day when their God would come and take them as His bride, and when once again much singing and dancing would be seen in the streets of Jerusalem.

She loved the seasons of harvest that correlated with the feasts of the Lord and knew that each one was important in the timeline of Yahweh's plan. She believed it was the season for the fulfillment of another chapter, and was dismayed that her people seemed to have become lax in their ability to discern the time that the prophets said a Redeemer would come to Zion.

Shoshana was so caught up in rehearsing the promises of God to her people that she went past her destination. Oh well, it wasn't that far. As she turned to retrace her steps, she noticed a group of men with a Rabbi in their midst ahead of her on the road. She saw the Rabbi walk to the side of the road and stand beside a fig tree, and before she knew it, the fig tree began to wither right there on the spot. She could not believe her eyes and moved closer to get a better look at what she had just witnessed. Why? Why did she see this fig tree wither before this Rabbi?

His disciples were speechless until one of them finally opened his mouth and said something. She could not hear the question, but comprehended by the answer that this Rabbi definitely knew the season for all things, especially the season of fruitfulness for the fig tree before Him. She remembered that the prophet Hosea said that when Yahweh saw Israel's forefathers, it was as the delight of seeing the early fruit on the fig tree. She again realized that so many of her people today were straying from the truth of their forefathers. Abraham, Isaac and Jacob gave up their own paths and walked the paths that were chosen by God himself. And the wives of these men, Shoshana thought, were as equal in faithfulness as their husbands. She looked up and saw that the disciples and the Rabbi had walked on toward the city.

Shoshana turned her attention back to the shopping she had come to do, but her mind was still preoccupied with what she had witnessed on the road. She entered the frenzied atmosphere of the marketplace and was instantly swept into the current of people pushing and bumping and stepping on toes. Soon she was hearing the loud voices of the vendors competing for priority in the ears of the shoppers. She had concluded long ago that they must do it for their own entertainment because the shoppers paid no attention to them. Shoppers had their own methods of determining the best quality and price, which usually involved competitions between themselves. For instance, if Shlomo said "these" were the best figs, then Noach said "those" were the best figs and a feisty argument ensued. They were probably best friends, but each one "had to be right" and had to try to convince the other of that fact. It's just the way it is, and in the end, everyone goes home happy.

Shoshana thought she would go the long route to her home which took her through the grove of olive trees outside the city wall. As she was admiring the beauty of these ancient trees, she again recognized the Rabbi and His disciples. The disciples had crowded around the Rabbi and were listening so intently that Shoshana again drew closer in order to eavesdrop. She found a large olive tree with low growing bushes that she hoped would hide the brilliant blue robe she was wearing today. As she settled her shoulders down into the massive trunk of the olive tree, she fit so perfectly into it that she thought she must look like one of the actual branches protruding from its trunk. She felt at peace and was thankful for the secret hideaway that enabled her to hear what the Rabbi was saying.

The Rabbi began to teach that a fig tree is a sign of the end times. She couldn't believe what she was hearing, especially after what she had witnessed happen to the fig tree that had withered earlier this morning. She heard Him say and could understand enough to know that they were to look for the tender twigs and the sprouting of its leaves. She heard the season of summer spoken of and then she heard the words, "It is near, right at the door." All of a sudden, Shoshana's shoulder slipped from the spot that she had leaned into and was now firmly lodged in the olive tree. She was stuck! She gasped, and as she let out a squeal, the Rabbi looked up at her, and in that glance, she knew He was the True Messiah she had been waiting for who filled all the seasons of Israel with life and hope.

Thoughts To Meditate On:

Will you and I be in the right season? Will we recognize the season of His coming? When we begin to excavate our heritage in the Messiah Yeshua, we find there are seasons of Feasts laid out before us to rehearse and to put the words He has spoken to us into action, to remind us of Who He is and of the time He will come to receive us into His Presence. How wonderful that His People Israel kept alive the Feasts for you and me as Messianic Gentiles, to watch and behold His Word coming to pass right before our eyes!

We have emerged into the Light of His Presence and have begun to understand as Messianic Gentiles where we fit into the Olive Tree. I know for so long in my own life I was in a winter season, not realizing that I could be released into the Spring. Then I finally realized I was invited to partake of the sap from the Olive tree and become mature. I sought after the Holy Spirit for the rain of His Presence, not just at the altar of the church, but every day. I would cry out for more of His rain to be released in my life so that the Seed of His Word could now be received into the soft soil of my heart.

As I pursued the Lord in the Word that He gave us, I saw the Feasts that He laid out before us as a path of truth and security for all believers to adhere to. That as we stay within the seasons of the Feasts, they become a safety net to reveal where our hearts are with Him and also to reveal the nearness of His coming. He is the Feasts of the Lord, our Yeshua! When we acknowledge and participate in the Feasts of the Lord, we are in the perfect will of His heart for us to be ready for His return. As we anticipate each feast and realize that we are now partakers and not just spectators, there is no fear of being left behind because each feast reminds us of His soon appearance. I challenge you to study the seven feasts of the Lord that will bring a completed picture of the whole olive tree and who He is, the Glory of Israel.

My heart's cry for all people who worship the God of Abraham, Isaac, and Jacob, who gave us His beloved son, Yeshua, is that we would arise and enter into the springtime of our journey and behold the fig tree that has blossomed.

Scripture To Know And Store In Our Hearts:

<u>Proverbs 27:18</u> *"He who tends a fig tree will eat its fruit, and he who looks after his master will be honored."*

<u>Song of Songs 2:11-13</u> *"For lo, the winter is past, the rain is over and gone. The flowers appear on the earth; the time of singing has come, and the voice of the turtledove is heard in our land. The fig tree puts forth her green figs, and the vines with the tender grapes give a good smell. Rise up, my love, my fair one, and come away!" NKJV*

<u>Hosea 9:10</u> *"When I found Israel, it was like finding grapes in the desert; when I saw your fathers, it was like seeing the early fruit on the fig tree."*

<u>Matthew 21:18-19</u> *"Early in the morning, as he was on his way back to the city, he was hungry. Seeing a fig tree by the road, he went up to it but found nothing on it except leaves. Then he said to it, 'May you never bear fruit again!' Immediately the tree withered." (May we be found with fruit on our branches.)*

<u>Mark 13:28-31</u> *"Now learn this lesson from the fig tree: As soon as its twigs get tender and its leaves come out, you know that summer is near. Even so, when you see these things happening, you know that it is near, right at the door. I tell you the truth, this generation will certainly not pass away until all these things have happened. Heaven and earth will pass away, but my words will never pass away."*

Prayer of Revelation:

Dear Abba, Father,

Help us to understand the current season of Your people Israel and to know that You call us to be one with Your family and to stand right there with them in this season. Help us to be faithful to Your Word and to Your covenant with Your people Israel. Help us to arise and come away into Your Presence and to sit underneath the fig tree. As we partake of Your ordained feasts, may our eyes and ears be opened to hear what the Spirit is saying concerning Your people Israel. Open our hearts to the words of prophecy from Your prophets, and may we, as one voice in each appointed feast, join with the song of welcome for Your return. Even as Pesach comes around the corner each year, may we come around the corner and greet You, the Passover Lamb, who arrived in the springtime to give new life to those who cried "Blessed is He that comes in the name of the Lord!"

Amen.

Tamar – One Day He Will Come

Tamar had a heaviness in her heart that she could not shake off. She knew what it was all about, but to voice it would be too much for her tender heart. She had felt the glances of the townspeople and heard the whispers about her. How she tried to keep her head held high without falling prey to her weaknesses. She knew what they were saying, and deep inside, she did long to have a wedding day that would be her own. She would dream about it through the night hours and then awake exhilarated until she realized it was just that – a dream.

There was much to be thankful for. She had a wonderful family who loved her. Tamar was the only girl in the family, surrounded by brothers who were all married. She had cast upon the ground many flower petals for her brothers' wives as their day under the chuppah came. And Tamar also had been diligent in getting herself ready for the heavenly day of her own wedding, mostly subconsciously, not fully realizing how strong her desire for it really was. Tamar had taken care of her body for the day she would give herself away in abandonment to her husband. She understood that she had to love herself first before she could give herself wholly to another. Tamar counted the days, knowing that each one brought her that much closer to finding her love. One day she, too, would walk upon the petals of orange blossoms and be engulfed in the arms of her beloved.

This morning, though, she pushed aside her thoughts of a husband and decided to drink in the beauty of the land to satisfy her soul. Tamar decided she would go for a walk in the hills of Judea surrounding her dwelling place. She breathed deeply the aroma of the jasmine flowers that permeated the early morning air.

Tamar stayed deep within her thoughts, not realizing that someone was walking toward her. Unaware of her whereabouts, she bumped into a figure on the path. Startled, she looked up and saw herself gazing into the most beautiful, brown eyes she had ever seen. They seemed to pour forth volumes of beautiful words with just a look. Catching herself longing to drink deeply from these eyes, the stranger greeted her with "Shalom, peace be unto you." Then, as suddenly as he had appeared to her on the path, he was gone.

Until that moment, she had believed that she was the only one who even knew of this hidden path on these beautiful hills around Jerusalem. Not everyone wanted the kind of solitude that Tamar embraced. This path knew every word that had ever come forth from her heart. It had become a scroll etched with her deepest desires, rolled out upon the earth, and only she and the path knew her secrets. But she had a sense that this stranger had somehow read her heart words as he walked upon this secret scroll.

A quick glance over her shoulder revealed the back of his tallit, glistening with sunbeams dancing on tassels that hung down his thighs. It was obvious from the garments he wore that he was a rabbi, but why did she get the feeling that he knew her from the inside out? She had never met a rabbi who made her react this way. How silly to feel such emotion from someone she only indirectly met on her private path.

Tamar began to shiver. It was not cold, but she felt something different today. Not only had the path recorded her words on its scroll, she also felt the winds of Jerusalem engulf her thoughts and carry them to the Temple Mount to be deposited in its secret chamber which held God's presence.

She longed for the fulfillment of the prophets' words that spoke of their Messiah who would come and walk amongst her people,

Israel. Her grandmother would say, "One day, He will come" not skipping a beat as she rolled out the dough for the family's daily bread. Tamar began to wonder if the words, "One day, He will come," were just the wishful thoughts of those who struggled to stay alive trying not to make a fuss for fear of the Roman soldiers. These days, it seemed that Roman soldiers were waiting at every corner to harass her people just because of their belief in a God that no one has seen. The Romans had many visible gods that were made of nothing but common stone. But her people believed that the God of Abraham, Isaac and Jacob was visible to them in their hearts, and that anyone could plainly see Him if only they would open their eyes within to see.

In her short time here on this earth, she made a point to study people. Human nature caused them to try to live up to what was expected of them by other people. She especially saw this in the women of her own family, who were fearful of what was being said about them by their neighbors (and vice-versa), but yet who all freely gave their pious smiles as they passed in the street. It was horrible what they spoke behind the backs of others, especially of those less fortunate than themselves. For example, they maliciously gossiped about a poor woman in the village because she had a bleeding problem that stopped her will to live. How sad that these women could betray another in a painful state that she has no control over. If only they would realize that, with hearts joined together for good, a minyan of women would be as powerful as a minyan of men. But Tamar knew that if she ever spoke this out, she, too, would be shunned, not because of a physical flowing of unclean blood, but because she had violated the rules of the rabbis with of her views on freedom for each and every woman in Israel. Freedom to live their life in the fullness and joy of Adonai.

She remembered a story in the Holy Scrolls that celebrated one woman's courageous spirit for speaking words of strength to another woman to be fearless and to stand up for her rights as a woman. The story was of Ruth, a Moabitess, who followed Naomi's instructions to reach out for a man of Bethlehem named Boaz.

Naomi convinced Ruth of who she was and that every woman should go to the threshing floor to find their Boaz.

Tamar began to blush as she recalled the story of the night that Ruth laid beneath the stars at the feet of Boaz, the perfumed oils of sweet flowers upon her body permeating the air with the fragrance that would arouse a man to take a woman into his arms and have her melt into his flesh as one. Yet, because of Boaz's heart for God, she knew he would wait for the hand of God to open the chamber of consecration for their night of ecstasy. It was as though Boaz knew all along that he would recognize the fragrance of the woman that his God had chosen for him. And he did. There was no mistaking the delicious scent that cascaded over Boaz like a waterfall. It was the very same scent of the woman who saturated his dreams. He awoke to the fragrance of that one in Ruth as she lay at his feet. He knew in an instant that she was to be his bride.

Tamar had also heard that the sages believed that even before time began, God created each soul to fit together with another specific soul, and that these two souls would perfectly complete each other with pure love and devotion. They were "meant to be" together. Unfortunately, it was obvious to Tamar that many marriages were arranged for the sake of convenience, or worse yet, because of another family's reputation. A family must always seek to attain a higher status in the village. Tamar believed it was nothing more than a caste system, with people's lives forced into man-made standards. What must their God think of them that they had wandered so far from His purposes and had diminished their standards to those of the other nations, yet tried to disguise it with a smug self-righteousness?

Tamar hoped a rabbi would come forth who would place himself as an advocate for women in the family of God, that they would be recognized as gifts to be treasured by the men in the community. A rabbi who would take a stand for righteousness in defense of the women who bear the offspring of Israel for the continuance of the Almighty's plan that Israel would be the light to the nations and that the Messiah would be one of their own. Tamar believed with everything in her that the real reason men place rules on women is to hide the fact that they fear the power of a woman who knows her God.

Tamar knew that her Creator stood to redeem Eve back from her deception even as He redeemed Adam. Truly, did not God do that for Eve in the garden, even after she was the one who offered the forbidden fruit to Adam and caused both to sin? Did not God also redeem her back as He redeemed Adam back by calling for both of them and asking, "Where are you?" Was not Eve's nakedness covered with the same animal skin that covered Adam? Did not God himself cover both of them with the sacrifice that shed its blood to give them a garment? Did not God Himself proclaim over Eve that her offspring would crush the serpent's head?

Tamar could not understand how the hearts of her beloved community, of her beloved Israel, had become so dulled to the beautiful aroma of the women in their midst, when it was Lord Himself who had prophesied the victory that the offspring of a woman would bring as head crusher of the serpent. She would giggle to herself when the Torah reading in the synagogue was the scripture that spoke Eve's words, "With the help of the Lord I have brought forth a man." She giggled because Eve did not even give Adam any credit at all in the creation of her offspring. But Tamar knew that if any rabbi heard her speak this out loud, she would certainly be shunned by the elders in her community. How often she wanted to ask questions and discuss scripture, but was held silent with a stern look from her brothers. But she began to recognize that when thoughts like this began stirring in her, something was about to take place in her life. Sometimes the multitude of her thoughts were exhausting, yet at the same time brought anticipation and exhilaration. She wished her people could feel this same exhilaration and realize that their purpose was to live and rejoice in the goodness of their God.

Tamar always kept her heart ready for the next turn that her life may take, and she had never been apprehensive about what surprise was in store for her around the next corner. She trusted what her God had prepared for her. She knew in her heart she was prepared to be a bride to her special someone, and that her special someone was already on the same path looking for her. Just as she had unexpectedly bumped into the rabbi with the deep brown eyes, so she would bump into her bridegroom-to-be.

Sometimes she amazed herself how, even in the complex world she lived in, she understood that life, in general, was simple if only people looked where they were stepping and which path they chose to be on. She had chosen to be on the path of preparation for each day that arrived, and also extended that preparation for the days ahead. Tamar not only waited for the Messiah to come and rescue her people, Israel, but she also waited for her bridegroom to come and sweep her into his arms and take her into that hidden chamber. Even as her people accepted the law at Mt. Sinai as a marriage contract, she had made herself ready to enter into a marriage contract with the man of her dreams. But she also knew that this season of preparation required the gift of patience to endure the waiting for the promise to be fulfilled.

That night at the evening meal, her father and brothers had a strange conversation that, of course, the women of the family were not invited to join into. They spoke of a rumor they had heard that day about a rabbi who had unknowingly made the Pharisees in the city angry at him. Her father said that the Pharisees were calling this rabbi from Nazareth a false teacher, one who opposed the law of Moses and openly broke the law with his followers. Tamar wanted to ask how one man had enough influence in this city of religious teachers to have caused this much talk. She knew that there was a history of many strange men with strange teachings declaring that they were the Messiah and to come and follow them. Yes, she had heard that, in fact, many people had been deceived and did follow these men, but always managed to find their way back home after being taken for all their money and belongings.

Then her brother said something that totally astounded her. He told a story that he had heard from Jacob the butcher, who had been told by Nathaniel the scholar, who heard it from

Shimron the tailor, who was the cousin of Mattaniah, who, as it turns out, personally knew the Pharisee who actually invited this rabbi for dinner at his home last night. This reputable Pharisee was known by everyone in the city of Jerusalem, and of course, he wanted everyone in the city to know of his piousness and his upstanding religious position in the community. But the evening held a surprise, not only for him, but one that now the whole city was talking about.

As was the custom of her people, the invited guests occupied seats at the host's table, but there were also benches set around the room against the walls for those who ate the leftover scraps from the meal. What really caught Tamar's attention was when her brother began to talk about a certain "unscrupulous woman" who was at the center of the narrative. As the story unfolded in Tamar's ears, she learned that the unscrupulous woman did a very strange thing. She had come forward from the outer circle holding an alabaster jar. She began crying at the feet of this rabbi and then wiped the tears from his feet with her hair. Then she kissed his feet and poured the expensive contents of the alabaster jar over the rabbi's feet.

Tamar could not believe what she was hearing as her heart melted into this unknown woman's actions of love for this rabbi who was causing such a stir in her city, Jerusalem. She herself wanted to know this rabbi and to be in his presence even as this unscrupulous woman had so dared to be. Surely the words "courageous" and "bold" should have been spoken of her instead of the words "unclean" and "sinner" that had been placed upon her by the religious men of the city. Tamar's heart began to beat faster as she remembered her secret hope for a rabbi like this – One who would defend a woman who knelt in desperation to be clean and whole.

Her older brother, Uzziah, interrupted her younger brother, Nahshon, to tell what happened next and how the rabbi's incredible words pierced all who were there. The rabbi began to teach Simon the Pharisee of love and forgiveness and that this woman exemplified the elements of washing – the kiss, the oil, the power of forgiveness and love. Even as her brother said these words, the very essence of the drama that had taken place across town last night suddenly filled their own home. The men of the house became silent as they knew their words of judgment were nullified by the rabbi's words and love toward this woman. Tamar realized that tonight at their evening meal, her family had heard something that was beyond the natural love of a man for a woman, but it was a love that could only come from their God, the God of Abraham, Isaac and Jacob. But who was this rabbi that defied man's attempt and failure to love only with words but not with the heart?

The last words from her brother left them motionless as he relayed to them the words of the rabbi over the woman. The rabbi said, "Your sins are forgiven. Your faith has saved you; go in peace." Again, her father and brothers could not even refute or give their opinion as men usually do when it comes to the rules and regulations of a rabbi's actions toward a woman that others had walked away from. They all sat for what seemed like an eternity, contemplating the implications of what they had just heard. The atmosphere was thick, yet holy, and for the longest time, no one moved from the table. Her mother finally rose and began to clear the table, which was a sign to Tamar to gather herself and to begin the evening routine of preparing the meal for the morning. No more words were spoken that night.

Tamar awoke with an awareness that something in the atmosphere had changed, but couldn't put her finger on exactly what it was. She just knew that the city of Jerusalem would never be the same again – or was it just herself that had changed during the night hours? Her body felt warm, as though it held slow burning coals that caused her to glow from the inside out. She wondered if anyone else could see it. She made her way to the marketplace to buy her favorite cinnamon sticks and say hello to the shopkeeper. The Jerusalem breeze cooled her face as she walked, but the coals were still burning inside her vessel. What a strange sensation she was experiencing today.

It was a beautiful day. Along the road, she attempted to count the first flowers that had burst through the earth's surface to eagerly spread their petals to the warmth of the sun. What is it about springtime that always brings happiness and love to the city of Jerusalem? Who was it, anyway, that determined that springtime would be the season that lovers would secretly touch each other's hands in the marketplace, or that their looks of secret desire would be more evident for all to see? Was it because the earth was awakened to release its love to the inhabitants dwelling on its surface? Tamar thought to herself that this must be a glimpse of what the Garden of Eden was like every day before the fall of the two lovers took place.

This beautiful season would be the perfect time to travel up to the Galilee to visit with her mother's sister, Aunt Mahlah, who always loved on her and spoke such beautiful things about her life in the midst of the Gentiles along the sea of Galilee. Aunt Mahlah was a beautiful woman who exuded femininity in every aspect of her life. She always told Tamar, "Wait for the man who will upset your heart with love and will turn your thoughts into sweet honey every time you think of him." She then would whisper to Tamar, "Do not let anyone else choose the man for you to marry; only you must choose the man that you want to have hold you in his arms for the rest of your life." Then the twinkle in her Aunt's eyes would dance like fire because she herself had stood before her parents and said 'No' to their choice of a husband for her. The man they had chosen for her had a prosperous export business selling Galilee fish to the neighboring lands, but she did not choose to sleep with an abundance of fish in her bed.

Tamar could not restrain herself from totally losing control at her aunt's humor, not that she tried very hard. The laughter would involuntarily bubble up and gush out of her, and she would laugh till she cried and it felt so good to have such a joyous release. It was amazing to her how some people could just make you feel so comfortable and free to be yourself.

Aunt Mahlah had married a wonderful man who treated her

like a princess. He provided her with the desire of her life, and that was to truly love and be loved. One night, he reached out and touched her tenderly as if he seemed to know that this was the last touch to his princess, and then quietly took his last breath. Her aunt was now a widow, but the smile and contentment on the face of this once-passionate bride was as if she still occupied the wedding chamber with the love of her life.

The journey would take two days, so she convinced one of her brothers that he needed to go to the Galilee for business. He consented to let her "tag along" with him, provided she heeded his instruction to keep silent and not ask thousands of questions as they went. Her brother was a man of silence, and wanted those around him to have the same attitude. But he had a soft spot that Tamar knew exactly how to get to, and she knew she would succeed in getting him to talk with her all the way to the Galilee. She smiled to herself.

The first day of travel took them through the Jordan valley, which had a special beauty that Tamar loved to take in. The Jordan valley was a dangerous place to travel because of the wild animals that inhabited the dense vegetation along its shores. They stopped for the night and knew the place that they set up their small tent would be safe from the four-footed animals and even the two-footed ones that had turned bad and were always looking for prey to feed their corrupted souls. Tamar slept well, knowing she was safe with the servants who traveled with them and with her brother who was a well-equipped man physically.

Waking up to the morning sun, the next day would have them pass through Tiberias, Magdala, and then finally to Capernaum where her aunt lived along the shores in a beautiful dwelling surrounded by wildflowers. Everything in the Galilee seemed to be alive and was declaring the beauty of God's creation. Tamar couldn't wait to get to her aunt's house and once again sit on the shore where she always heard the waves speaking to her of the wonders of her God. She began to recognize the stones that had been set up by those who lived in the area to direct travelers to their destination. They were allowed to pass through, but the land was owned by those who toiled and brought forth the fruit of it.

As they crested the gentle slopes leading to her Aunt Mahlah's cottage along the sea, Tamar's five senses were touched by the sweeping scene before her: the sea and its brilliant color, the green meadows, the sound of the native birds welcoming each traveler, the lush jasmine bush that kissed her cheeks, and the inviting fragrance of the earth itself ascending into her nostrils as it spoke of its riches for those who lived here. She could even taste the freshness of the sea. Everything in her came alive.

There ahead was her Aunt Mahlah, framed by the sea waters as she stood against the backdrop of velvet blue, waving to Tamar as if the native birds had announced her coming to her aunt's ears. What an amazing place to live. Tamar wanted to rush into her aunt's open arms to receive the huge squeeze she knew awaited her. Her donkey, though, seemed to sense her anticipation and, being a donkey, chose this moment to slow to a leisurely stroll instead of accommodating its passenger's wishes. Tamar never kicked her donkey, but today was the day to let her beast know that she was the owner of its four legs. She prodded him, but realized he only picked up speed as he recognized aunt Mahlah and remembered that she always had a sweet handful of grain waiting for him.

Sliding off her donkey, Tamar was at once in the sweet smelling arms of her Aunt Mahlah and tangled in the colorful scarves that were wrapped around her once-slender, now very womanly body that had earned its extra folds by partaking of the sweet breads that she made for the poor who sat outside the synagogue entrance. Led into her aunt's dwelling, smelling the luscious soup brimming with vegetables, and of course her famous freshly baked sweet bread, Tamar was at home in the Galilee.

Awakened by the morning kiss of her aunt, she was softly instructed to rise and get dressed and put on her beautiful blue dress because they were going to go to the village to buy the latest imported silk from across the waters. Tamar embraced the adventurous spirit of her aunt and delighted in it because it was exactly what Tamar felt inside of herself. She had so loved the warm bath her aunt had prepared for her the evening before that held within its borders red rose petals. What a romantic her aunt was! Tamar's skin was soft and smooth to the touch and again she realized how thankful she was for a woman like Aunt Mahlah in her life. Womanhood reached its highest peak of perfection in her aunt, and Tamar had so much to learn from her.

Walking down the road to the village and coming close to the outskirts, they both noticed at the same time a crowd gathered around a Rabbi. Tamar actually felt sorry for the Rabbi who was being pressed by the people from every direction. Suddenly, the Rabbi turned and spoke to the crowd and said, "Who touched me?" Tamar and her aunt could not believe what they had just heard and turned and stared at each other with astonishment.

She overheard words coming from a man close to the Rabbi, but could not distinguish what he had said. Again, the Rabbi said, "Someone touched me; I know that power has gone out from me." What power was He talking about? Why would a power come from a person that was only a man? Yes, a man of religious position, but still only a man.

Hardly believing what they were seeing, a woman came forward and began to say she had touched Him and was healed of her constant bleeding. No one moved nor uttered a sound for what seemed to be forever. Finally, the Rabbi said, "Daughter, your faith has healed you. Go in shalom." The Rabbi looked up and his eyes met Tamar's and instantly she recognized He was the One who had said "Shalom" to her on her secret path outside of Jerusalem.

Her eyes were opened and she knew He was not just an ordinary man, but He was the One who had come to take the curse from all womankind, the descendants of their mother in the Garden of Eden, Eve herself. He was the Messiah that had come to say to all of the daughters of Israel, "Live!"

Thoughts To Meditate On:

Christian women all over the world, like Eve, have been deceived by words that are not true. Many times we have heard words that were said to have been God's words and we failed to research them for ourselves. Israel, as the bride, has been guaranteed a bridal contract by the Lord Himself, written in the Bible, that says she belongs to Him because she accepted His proposal at Mt. Sinai. There is a powerful scripture that clearly states the heart of God concerning his chosen people. Ezekiel 16:6 says, "Then I passed by and saw you kicking about in your blood, and as you lay there in your blood I said to you, 'Live!'"

As we read the words of the prophet Ezekiel, we see the story of the woman with the issue of blood. There are not any men on this earth, maybe with the exception of doctors, who want to hear about a woman's menstrual cycle. They become extremely uncomfortable, and the look on their face is read by the woman, "Do not talk about such things." Even in this modern world, as I teach the scripture and bring forth a truth about a woman's cycle of bleeding, men squirm in the congregation and think that this is an unclean thing. The Lord Himself wanted us to see that it goes beyond the natural, into the spiritual, if only we would listen to the Holy Spirit.

As the covenant of blood was shed for Israel and God sees her as clean beyond the realm of time, we as women of God, should be able to understand and see even more clearly than what man can reason. If we see the parallel of God's love to Israel and the redemption from her defilement, then we know He has also come to us as women, to uphold our position in the Kingdom that He reigns over.

I want to challenge you as women to take hold of the Rabbi's tallit and be cleansed of your unclean blood that has deceived you and held you as prisoners. Take His blood and become liberated, as He has and will liberate Israel, His bride. One day He will come, and all of Israel will say, as Yeshua prophesied in the Holy Scriptures, "Blessed is He that comes in the Name of the Lord." Make yourself ready for the Bridegroom to come and take you as His bride because of the grafting into His olive tree.

Scriptures To Know And Store In Our Hearts:

Ezekiel 16:6-14 "*Then I passed by and saw you kicking about in your blood, and as you lay there in your blood I said to you, 'Live!' I made you grow like a plant of the field. You grew up and developed and became the most beautiful of jewels. Your breasts were formed and your hair grew, you who were naked and bare. Later I passed by, and when I looked at you and saw that you were old enough for love, I spread the corner of my garment over you and covered your nakedness. I gave you my solemn oath and entered into a covenant with you, declares the Sovereign LORD, and you became mine. I bathed you with water and washed the blood from you and put ointments on you. I clothed you with an embroidered dress and put leather sandals on you. I dressed you in fine linen and covered you with costly garments. I adorned you with jewelry: I put bracelets on your arms and a necklace around your neck, and I put a ring on your nose, earrings on your ears and a beautiful crown on your head. So you were adorned with gold and silver; your clothes were of fine linen and costly fabric and embroidered cloth. Your food was fine flour, honey and olive oil. You became very beautiful and rose to be a queen. And your fame spread among the nations on account of your beauty because the splendor I had given you made your beauty perfect, declares the Sovereign Lord.*"

Matthew 23:39 "*For I tell you, you will not see me again until you say, 'Blessed is he who comes in the name of the Lord.'*"

Matthew 27:25 "*All the people answered, "Let his blood be on us and on our children!*" (author's emphasis on this scripture is not what we have been taught from the pulpit as a judgment to the offspring of Israel, instead, they prophesied life to the children of Israel to all generations.)*

Revelation 19:6-8 "*And I heard, as it were, the voice of a great multitude, as the sound of many waters and as the sound of mighty thunderings, saying, 'Alleluia! For the Lord God Omnipotent reigns! Let us be glad and rejoice and give Him glory, for the marriage of the Lamb has come, and His wife has made herself ready.' And to her it was granted to be arrayed in fine linen, clean and bright, for the fine linen is the righteous acts of the saints.*" NKJV

GLAD: Strong's Concordance 5463; chairo; to be "cheer"ful, i.e. Calmly happy or well off; farewell, be glad, God speed, greeting, hail, joy (fully), rejoice.

REJOICE: Strong's Concordance 21; agalliao; to jump for joy, i.e. exult:-be (exceeding) glad, with exceeding joy, rejoice (greatly)

HATH MADE HERSELF READY: Strong's Concordance 2090; hetoimazo; to prepare; prepare, provide, make ready.

Prayer of Revelation:

Oh, Abba Father,

How we thank You for Your love and grace to us by giving us Your beloved son, Yeshua, to save and redeem us from our own sins. We ask, Abba, that You would forgive us for not making ourselves ready in this hour, and that we would have the grace now to give You everything to make ourselves ready for Your Son, Yeshua.

Yeshua, we thank You and praise You for Your beautiful love towards us and Your desire for us to be Your bride. You have shown us Your covenant of unfailing love to Israel and You have kept Your covenant with her to sweep her into Your chamber of faithfulness.

Ruach HaKodesh, come upon us and bring revelation of "One day He will come." Show us how to stay "happy" in Your presence and to ask You what we need in this hour to be the bride of the Messiah, Yeshua.

We give You our ears to hear and we give You our hearts to respond to Your words. We are marrying a Jewish bridegroom. Teach us how to become one with Your words of instruction in this hour so we will be ready and waiting to hear the shofar sound.

Amen.

Lydia – The Jewish Messiah

Awakened late at night by a stirring within, Lydia arose from her bed, the light of the New Moon coming through her window. She knew the Stranger had arrived once more to knock on the door of her passionate heart, which was now pounding with anticipation. As her feet slipped to the floor, she suppressed the passion to a low ember, not allowing her breath to spark a fire with the words, "Will this be the night?" Very slowly, she walked through the chamber and stopped before the door of her heart. Lydia gazed at her own heart through the latticed window grafted onto its frame. It stood out as an arched gate. She saw the silhouette of the One who patiently stood, longing for her to open the door this night.

On so many nights, too many to be numbered, this Stranger of kindness stood outside the door of her heart, desiring to be welcomed in. Lydia saw the fullness of His beard, the strength in the arch of His nose, the deep rich color of His hair by the glow of the moonlit night. As the light of the moon cascaded down upon Him, she embraced with her eyes the strength of His shoulders and the beauty of His robe that radiated with an amber glow. And she admired the exquisite tallit that was draped over His royal frame. She knew in her limited understanding that His prayer shawl was a message of hope and promises, not only to the Jewish people, but also to her as a Gentile. In her heart she knew His Name was knotted in the tassels that hung down upon His thigh.

Lydia became aware that He was waiting for her to come underneath the covering of His prayer shawl for protection and safety. She found herself melting into His love that reached out to shield her in His Name. So many times she had seen Jewish men shelter themselves beneath their tallits to pray and seek to be alone with their Jewish God. She, too, longed to be shielded beneath the prayer shawl of the One who would love her. Lydia knew this One was the Jewish Messiah, but would He become her Messiah, too? She was a Gentile who longed to belong to His family. Would He love her as He loved His own people? Would she be welcomed into a culture that she knew nothing about? Would He teach her of His ways so she could become a family member with His people and become one with them? Should she trust her own longing and open the door of her heart to let the Holy One of Israel in so He could teach her to walk the Ancient Paths of His people Israel? Lydia woke up dazed from the dream once again. Each night the dream would reoccur and ignite her secret passion of wanting to be loved and cared for.

As a Gentile, Lydia knew how far away she was from this Holy One. She had observed the Jewish people cling with joy and desperation to this One who had saved them from the hot furnace of Egypt. Lydia heard so many times from her family that the Israelites were different and that they worshiped only one God, but her people had many gods. She was, however, given the freedom to choose which god or gods she wanted to worship. Her family's home was littered with little icons of animals and people or combinations thereof. She found it so frightening, but was afraid to tell her father for fear of being scolded and reprimanded.

Lydia knew in her heart she was not like her family. Sometimes she would dream of climbing the stairs to the Jewish temple, revealing to those around her that she had a special invitation from the "Holy One" who dwelled inside the massive Temple. Just as she was about to enter the huge gate, she would awaken and find herself longing for the dream to continue.

Lydia knew that there was a great valley of differences between her people and the Israelites, but deep within she felt she would one day cross over and stand with hands lifted to worship the Invisible

God of the Israelites. But could it really be possible? If it did happen, she knew she would be cast out of her family and disowned from the wealth of their long-standing name. But somehow she also knew that the wealth which now surrounded her would one day become dusty and tattered, fading away with the passing of time. Lydia secretly desired to reach out for a relationship that would take her to the unseen world where the Creator of the Universe would call her by name.

She tried to shake these thoughts from her mind as she went about her errands for the day. But like the huge stones that made the Temple immovable, her thoughts would not move either. Maybe they were there because she often wondered if anybody truly cared about her. But every once in a while, when she felt she could not go on with life, it would suddenly seem as though there was someone who was reading her thoughts and she would begin to feel safe for no reason. Instantly a warm wave would flood over her as if Someone sitting in the heavens was pouring warm oil down upon her head and it was being soaked in by her own desire. It didn't make sense. It must be the soup she had eaten in the marketplace for lunch. That is it, she concluded. There must have been something that did not agree with her that made her think such outrageous things!

Lydia felt the heat of the day beating down upon her until little drops of sweat began to emerge on her brow. She looked down at the sandals on her delicate feet and decided that today she would buy new ones. Why not? Her father was wealthy, and he loved for her to show off his wealth with the lovely garments that she so beautifully wore to advertise his shops. He would beam with pride when she arrived home with lovely new sandals that complemented the garments he had designed and woven in his shop. Her father's shop was the most distinguished, expensive vendor shop in all of Jerusalem. Always, in the mercantile business, the most desirable shop was at the farthest end of the row. You had to be determined to push through the multitudes to reach it so you could purchase a unique garment that would stand out in a crowd. That was her father's shop.

She took pride in the fact that her father's exquisite colors were highly sought after. He trusted her with the formulas for the special dyes that were used on his rich fabrics. These precious secrets had been passed down through the family line and she felt very privileged to continue the family legacy. Although all their colors were beautiful, the one that the rich women of the upper city particularly favored was the color purple. So rich, so deep was the hue her father produced that people would even travel from far-away lands to buy bolts of the magnificently colored fabric.

Whenever these wealthy buyers would leave their shop, her father always turned to Lydia and said with a loud voice, "Be thankful, Lydia. You are a rich young woman of the city. This is where you are to count your blessings. The gods have blessed us with prosperity. We must give them an offering tonight and pay our respects." For some reason, these words never sat well in Lydia's heart, but she would tell herself that she should try to accept her life as it is.

Lydia's favorite shopping area was on the other side of the city. The street was known as "The Street of Sandaled Feet." She loved being waited on, and also relished the fact that many knew who she was and knew her family. Their name was renowned in the city. Lydia was sometimes ashamed of the attitude that she took on - the attitude of the rich – believing that they were above the poor, lowly servants who scurried about, doing errands for their Masters day and night. She argued with herself, trying desperately to justify her actions, repeating the words of her father that this is the life that the gods had designed for her. She was not a slave girl. She had all the time in the world to pamper herself.

Lydia noticed that it was especially busy today. There were so many more people in the streets than usual at this time of day. Many of them looked to have traveled long distances, with bundles slung over their shoulders, spilling over with "treasures" which could only be considered as such to those carrying them. Then she began to hear the murmur. Very quietly at first, and then the murmur rose to a shout, "He is over there!" She turned, and scanning the crowd, she locked eyes with the One they were shouting about. It was as though He was waiting for her to turn and look, like a magnet drawing her gaze to His. He smiled, and she felt as if the whole world would stop turning just to see His smile.

She knew he was Jewish by the way he looked, and his garments were those of a rabbi. How could he possibly stop in the midst of a crowd and notice her? But there was no doubt; He was smiling at her, a Gentile. Surely, He must see the difference in her style of dress and the jewelry she wore. Her heart began to pound, not with the pounding of a young maiden for a young man, but with a holiness that struck through her like a ray of light that flashes through a narrow opening.

What was happening? As though she was in a rehearsed scene and all the characters were in place, she began to hear the words, "Messiah, Messiah. Come and save us from the oppressor!" People were pushing to get to Him, to touch Him. She became frightened for fear of being trampled by the multitude. But all of a sudden, one of His followers took her hand and steadied her. He was a short, stocky man with the most penetrating gray eyes, but yet in an instant they brought comfort to her. She could see kindness and gentleness in the man's eyes as they concentrated on her fright. He looked like one who spoke little, but his actions were loud. She seemed to know somehow that he must be a scribe of many words. Lydia heard someone say over the noise of the crowd, "Yochanan, come, the Master needs you."

As quickly as it had begun, the whole scene was over before she could even comprehend it. She found herself asking, "What just happened?" Lydia could not even remember why she had come to this part of the city. Realizing she was standing motionless as people went about their business, she knew she had to continue her way and tried to put one foot in front of the other. She was trembling, but not like she would in the cold wind that chilled her bones in the winter months. It was a trembling that was delightful to every part of her being.

Before she took three steps, she realized that the One she had been having the dreams about was the One that smiled at her. Or was He? Lydia tried to remember with detail the look of His face, His robes, the arch of His nose, the beard that so neatly flowed down below His chin. Yes, she was certain, He was the One. What will her night of dreams be like tonight when she lays her head upon her pillow to enter into the unknown? She could hardly wait to arrive home and see the sunset that would signal it was time for sleep. This night will be like no other night for Lydia. She had met the Man of her dreams.

The next morning, Lydia decided to go to the open market. She knew that this was the job of the servant girls, but secretly she loved the atmosphere that surrounded her in the market. Her father always got so upset when he found out that she had done the servant girls' tasks, but he also always got over it. The disapproving look on her father's face would slowly fade away as he looked upon the beauty of his daughter, Lydia. The moment he gave up and shrugged his shoulders, she knew she had once again won him over.

There was a chill in the air this morning, but it did not permeate Lydia's warm, snug garments. The good news was that she saw the sun of Jerusalem peering through the gray clouds, and knew in her heart the sun would win out over the cold. Sure enough, Lydia opened her door and felt the sun's victory as it warmed her cheeks. Yes, this would be a good day in the city.

Lydia walked along the winding path with the smooth, worn cobblestones beneath her feet. Her mind began its ponderings again, and today it wondered whose feet had walked this path before and been a part of smoothing out the stones for her own feet to tread upon. She couldn't help it that her mind always went to such places. Her mother, who had passed away suddenly last year, would always say, "Lydia, you have to stop your daydreaming. It will bring you to a dead end." She missed her mother greatly, but did not miss the coldness that could come from her voice. Her father loved her openly and unconditionally, but her mother was more closed and never really knew how to give out her love.

The many silences between her father and mother were so thick you could cut them with a knife. Lydia became determined that her husband would be like her father, more sensitive, but that she would not be like her mother.

She did believe that somewhere deep within her mother there was a warm heart that was yearning to be released from its cold prison, but each time her mother would go and pray to the gods, she would come back the same. "How sad," Lydia would say to herself. These gods had been given so much by the people – even children to be burned upon their altars – and yet they could not unlock a woman's heart to experience joy for living. So many questions Lydia would have, but she knew that her mother never questioned anything about the gods. She just accepted what was given to her to believe.

Lydia finally arrived at the market and all her senses came alive. She smelled the piping hot sweet breads, heard the vendors shouting their prices, saw the fish from the Galilee flopping in their small container prisons. She observed the not-so-expensive robes hanging from hooks swaying in the gentle breeze, clay pots displayed in disarrayed fashion, and, of course, the abundant bags of spices that aroused the taste buds. What a wonderful place!

Her mother, when she was alive, would never come to the "shuk" because it was for those trying to save their shekels. Lydia's mother loved her way of life and was proud that she could go to the elegant spice shops of the upper city and be waited on. Not so for Lydia. She loved the sheer pleasure of living and being alive to experience every part of society. Lydia was determined that she would not become a snob of the city.

She reached out to taste a green olive and once again found herself in a larger-than-usual crowd, being pushed and shoved about. Just like that, she was thrown off her feet into a container of olives. How could people be so rude? Why did they have to act as though they were running from a fire? She was just minding her own business, trying to do her daily shopping. As she collected herself, looking around to see if anyone had noticed her unladylike predicament, she saw what the commotion was all about. It was the Rabbi again! She could see his silhouette in the sunlight and watched in amazement as He touched those who came to Him. He spoke with such authority, but also with such gentleness, like a soft breeze. Even the children flocked around Him, like little sheep around a shepherd. Old, young, rich, poor – He welcomed everyone. So complex this man from Nazareth, but yet she could see that even the simpleminded understood what He was saying.

She was surprised to see some Sadducees come forward out of the crowd and question Him. How odd, she thought. Wouldn't such learned men as they already know who He was? Lydia could not hear everything, but she did hear the Rabbi's answer. "I am the God of Abraham, the God of Isaac, and the God of Jacob. He is not the God of the dead, but of the living." People near her began talking about the amazing things He had being doing in the city. Apparently, every person this Rabbi touched was healed and set free from prisons of sickness, mental torment – all manner of things. She could tell from listening to the crowd that many Jews were asking "Who is this man?" But at the same time, many others were calling Him a prophet, a healer, a teacher – even going so far as to say, "He is the Mashiach who the prophets said would come and deliver us."

The crowd began to simmer down as the Rabbi had gone on His way with His disciples. She knew she would be late getting home, but she didn't care. It had been an incredible day in the shuk. But Lydia knew she must buy something to take home to her father. Otherwise, he would be asking too many questions as to her lateness. "Oh, I know," Lydia exclaimed out loud to herself, "Olives!" Surely the man would give her a good deal on them, and she would buy enough to pay him back for the damage. So on her way with green olives in hand, Lydia sang a lovely song under her breath, happy to have encountered the Rabbi again.

On arriving home, Lydia was surprised to see that there were some interesting guests with her father in the sitting room for visitors. She could tell the conversation was very serious by the deep lines etched in their brows. The more they talked, the deeper the lines became. Finally, her father looked up, greeted her with a warm kiss upon her forehead, and introduced her to the men. They were oblivious to the introduction and continued their conversation without pausing.

Lydia listened in since she could tell they didn't care or even see that she was there. She learned that they were all makers of the little icon-gods that the Gentiles purchased by the dozen. They were telling her father about a certain Man who had been damaging their livelihood. They said, "We asked ourselves, 'How can a Jewish Rabbi possibly damage our businesses?' Let us tell you why. Our people have been listening to this Man's silly words about salvation, redemption – 'Repent, follow Me and I will give you life.'" They explained that many Jews, Gentiles, and even some Roman soldiers believed that this Rabbi was the Mashiach of the Jews. And that some of their ancient scrolls had mentioned that this Holy One would also include the Gentiles in His salvation plan.

The more the men talked, the angrier they became. Her father kept trying to calm them down, saying, "Stop all this nonsense and fretting. This Man, too, will disappear just as all the other so-called Messiahs have." He reminded them of how many had come and gone in the last few years. Even in the last few months, many had come into the city with a big flash and were soon gone, never to be heard from again. "This Rabbi from Nazareth will be like all the rest. He, too, will come to the surface, but will disappear also."

The men, not seeming to be convinced, finally began to leave, muttering under their breath. Lydia sensed that they somehow felt this One was different. Why? Because the whole city was in a stir and this One was making waves against the Sadducees and the Pharisees like no one else had ever done before. This One came as one of the people and loved the people. It was as if He was sent down from heaven, but yet was one of us. And He walked the laws of the Torah like no one else had ever done before. This Rabbi was showing the people how to not only talk the Torah, but also walk the Torah. He was showing the people that as you love God with all your heart, soul, and mind, that He would reveal Himself to you.

After the men had left her home, Lydia looked at the bewilderment on her father's face and knew that this Rabbi had affected him, too. She knew her father had also overheard the patrons of his shop talking together and discussing the recent sayings of the Rabbi. She could tell he was paying attention because he would sway back and forth on his feet. He always did that when he was trying to act like he wasn't listening but really was. Especially when it came to the topic of religion. He had done that many times to her when she would try to talk to him about their beliefs. She would ask questions and he would act like he didn't hear her, swaying to some imaginary music in his head. She would even try to lure him into an argument, so at least he would tell her what was really in his heart. But he acted deaf because he loved her and did not want to argue. Lydia knew that, but deep down she also knew it was because he did not have the answers for her – or for himself. She did love her father.

Lydia slipped out of the room and left her father with his thoughts. She was tired and had her own thoughts to mull over. Maybe tonight she would once again encounter the Knight in shining armor who loved her in her dreams.

The next morning Lydia was drawn to the Temple that Herod had built for the Jewish people. Her heart was leading her in a way she had never experienced before. Yes, she did dream about the Rabbi. He told her in the dream that He was the Way, Truth and Life. She did not know what those words meant, but in her dream she felt safe as she wrapped her heart around them. Just remembering her dream gave her a sense of belonging, but to whom or what people, she did not know. She did know the truth in her own heart that she wanted to belong to the Rabbi and His disciples, which included all people of every race and color.

She also was listening to the talk in her father's shop as some of the rich women whispered that they, too, had been following the Rabbi at a distance, but would have to be so careful not to be recognized by those who were spies. These days, it seemed that everyone was a spy for someone. Either a spy from the Great Sanhedrin or a spy from the pagan places where people would go and pay the priest to pray to a god, any god that was available.

She came to believe that this Rabbi walked in a peace she had never seen anyone walk in before. But there were predictions that one day He would go too far, and words like "stoned" or "accidentally pushed over a cliff" were being said. She hoped in her heart that He would never die, but would continue to live amongst the people of Jerusalem forever. She felt unworthy for these thoughts to parade across her mind as if they knew they had a right to be there.

Today was the Jewish Sabbath day of worship and the synagogues were full. She liked to peek in and listen to the reading of their large scrolls. Lydia knew that if she stopped now, she would not have time to walk to the Temple. But the joyous sounds flowing out from the nearby synagogue drew her as a bee to the honeycomb. As she ventured up the steep climb, she could not believe her ears. It was His voice. She was so glad they had kept the door open that day, even though the winter wind of Jerusalem was present. As she looked in, she saw a woman who looked like she had been stooped over for many years of her life. The Rabbi motioned to her to come to Him. Every emotion imaginable was displayed on the faces of the people – scowls, bewilderment, apprehension – and a few smiles. She heard the Rabbi say, "Be free." Those were the only two words she heard, but that was enough. The woman began to straighten up as if she had merely bent down to pick something up from the floor and had been able to walk upright all her life. The woman began to shout praises to God, and to twirl and dance with excitement. She became like a banner spinning in the wind as though she would not allow anyone to fold her up again.

Needless to say, it caused quite a stir. Lydia heard the angry voices of the synagogue rulers saying, "Why on the Sabbath and not on the other days of the week?" Then everyone began shouting at once. The Rabbi responded with many words, but Lydia only clearly heard Him say, "Daughter of Abraham."

As He said these words, the Rabbi looked through the crowd directly at Lydia with His piercing eyes of love. For a moment, she thought He actually looked like a living Holy Scroll rolling itself out as a red carpet for her to walk upon. She was overcome with emotion. She melted. He was her answer. His eyes spoke words of life to her. Unspoken words, but words that firmly planted themselves in the deep, soft soil of her heart – words that welcomed her into His family and proved that His love reached to all people who would receive Him. Lydia knew that she finally belonged to a family that would teach her to walk the Ancient Paths of Israel.

Lydia wondered what the future held for the Rabbi who extended this extravagant love to all people. Some had told her that He would die to give His people life. Her heart could not accept these words. But someone had also told her that if a kernel of wheat does not die in the ground, then it cannot produce a harvest in due season. She did not understand what all of this meant. One thing she did finally understand, however, was that all the metal icons and wooden statues were dead objects made by human hands. But the Rabbi from Nazareth was sent from God Himself.

Thoughts To Meditate On:

We, as non-Jews, must begin to understand how blessed we are because of the demonstration of the Messiah of Israel also dying for us. I think that most of us do not take the time to stop and think about this subject. In the story of Lydia, she opened her heart to hear the truth, though it was foreign language to her ears. We, the church (called out ones) gladly receive salvation and a redeemed life that the death and resurrection of Yeshua gives to us, but we never stop long enough in our walk to know who He is and where He was born, lived, died and rose. Do we know the language of the One we love? He spoke Hebrew and Aramaic. Do we know what holidays He celebrated? Do we know what clothing He wore and why? Do we accept that salvation came from the Jews and not from non-Jews? Do we understand that now that we have received mercy from the Lord, we are to show mercy to His family?

Most of us have grown up in the Christian church where we have

Christmas pageants, Lenten services, and Easter egg hunts. Does Yeshua (Jesus) have anything at all to do with these Christian holidays? If He is the One who came to save us from our sins and died on Calvary to give us life, then why have we added holidays He never took part in nor spoke of? We, as non-Jews, need to understand that we are grafted into His Olive Tree; He is not grafted into our Christian Tree.

I often wondered why we were called in Romans 11:17 "wild olive branches," but after much meditation, I have come to the conclusion that Paul used the right description to paint a picture of who we are and that we were at one time separated from the commonwealth of Israel. The apostle Paul, I believe, was actually gentle with his description of us, the non-Jews. We are "wild" because we have not been taught the Hebraic Ways of the Jewish Bible. We have tried to make the Word of God fit our Gentile ways of life. This must be stopped for the sake of the Kingdom of God! Lydia knew the cost of turning away from pagan ways and clinging to the Messiah from Nazareth. She knew that everything she had been taught in her religion had to be left behind and she had to become a student (talmida) of the Savior Yeshua.

Ephesians 2:19-22 says, "So then, you are no longer foreigners and strangers. On the contrary, you are fellow-citizens with GOD'S PEOPLE and members of God's family. You have been built on the foundation of the emissaries and the prophets, with the cornerstone being Yeshua the Messiah himself. In union with him the whole building is held together, and it is growing into a holy temple in union with the Lord. Yes, in union with him, you yourselves are being built together into a spiritual dwelling-place for God." CJB

When a young woman falls in love with her husband-to-be, because she wants to love and honor him, she chooses to love what he loves, celebrate what he celebrates, and do what he loves to do. She is his bride. Does it take a while to conform to his time schedule, his ways of life? Yes! Is the husband patient with her? Yes, because he sees her love for him and he knows she wants to please him. The church that has accepted Yeshua and has said yes to Him should be the same way in our love for Him. We need to be equally yoked with the Lord, in agreement with Him and His ways, not having a tug a war because of wanting *to do things our own way.*

Even the first century Jewish Apostles knew that accepting these new non-Jewish believers into their families would be hard for some of their own Jewish brothers to accept. But through much prayer, and much love and understanding, they set guidelines for the non-Jews to follow. They knew that it would take diligent teaching and being an example themselves to show the Goyim (Gentiles) how to walk in "The Way." They were aware of the fact that their people were chosen to be a banner to the rest of the world of the God of Abraham, Isaac, and Jacob, and that they had a few thousand years' head start in knowing how to walk in His ways. When Yeshua came to them, He was revealed as the Written Word of Instruction, to show them how to live in the world, but not be of the world.

We must understand that it is we, the non-Jews, who convert to their Holy Word - not the other way around. They are already standing on the bedrock of the faith and have kept the Sacred Writings of the Word of God. It is now their turn to accept the Messiah Yeshua as they see us worshiping, not with foreign idol worship, but with the Hebraic worship of the Word of God.

What a challenge it is for us who were molded to the thoughts and actions of the Western World. The Way, the Truth and the Life came out of Israel. Let us embrace and be molded to His Words of life and truth. The clocks in our hearts should be set to the time zone of Israel, not the time zone of the West. Our thinking should be in one accord with the Holy Spirit who came to the brothers and sisters that were waiting for the Promise of the Father in the Upper Room.

We have so much to learn. But how exciting it is to love the Bridegroom and prepare ourselves for Him. He will know His bride when He comes for her because she has prepared herself for Him alone. Let us acknowledge that it is "We, the church" that needs to conform to Yeshua – not Yeshua that needs to conform to us.

Scriptures To Know And Store In Our Hearts:

<u>Romans 11:17-18</u> " *But if some of the branches were broken off, and you—a wild olive—were grafted in among them and have become*

equal sharers in the rich root of the olive tree, then don't boast as if you were better than the branches! However, if you do boast, remember that you are not supporting the root, the root is supporting you." CJB

<u>Ephesians 2:19-22</u> *"So then, you are no longer foreigners and strangers. On the contrary, you are fellow-citizens with GOD'S PEOPLE and members of God's family. You have been built on the foundation of the emissaries and the prophets, with the cornerstone being Yeshua the Messiah himself. In union with him the whole building is held together, and it is growing into a holy temple in union with the Lord. Yes, in union with him, you yourselves are being built together into a spiritual dwelling-place for God." CJB*

<u>Isaiah 42:6</u> *"I, ADONAI, called you righteously, I took hold of you by the hand, I shaped you and made you a covenant for the people, to be a light for the Goyim." CJB*

<u>Isaiah 49:6</u> *"It is not enough that you are merely my servant to raise up the tribes of Ya'akov and restore the offspring of Isra'el. I will also make you a light to the nations, so my salvation can spread to the ends of the earth." CJB*

<u>Luke 2:29-32</u> *"Now, ADONAI, according to your word, your servant is at peace as you let him go; for I have seen with my own eyes your yeshu'ah, which you prepared in the presence of all peoples—a light that will bring revelation to the Goyim and glory to your people Isra'el." CJB*

<u>Acts 9:15-16</u> *"But the Lord said to him, 'Go, because this man is my chosen instrument to carry my name to the Goyim, even to their kings, and to the sons of Isra'el as well. For I myself will show him how much he will have to suffer on account of my name.'" CJB*

<u>Acts 10:45-46</u> *"All the believers from the Circumcision faction who had accompanied Kefa (Peter) were amazed that the gift of the Ruach HaKodesh (Holy Spirit) was also being poured out on the Goyim, for they heard them speaking in tongues and praising God." CJB*

<u>Acts 11:1-3</u> *"The emissaries and the brothers throughout Y'hudah (Judah) heard that the Goyim had received the word of God; but when Kefa went up to Yerushalayim (Jerusalem), the members of the*

Circumcision faction criticized him, saying, 'You went into the homes of uncircumcised men and even ate with them!'" CJB

Acts 11:18 "On hearing these things, they stopped objecting and began to praise God, saying, 'This means that God has enabled the Goyim as well to do t'shuvah (turn around, repent) and have life!'" CJB

Acts 13:47,48 "For that is what ADONAI has ordered us to do: 'I have set you as a light for the Goyim, to be for deliverance to the ends of the earth.'" " The Gentiles were very happy to hear this. They honored the message about the Lord, and as many as had been appointed to eternal life came to trust." CJB

Acts 15:14-18 "'Shim'on (Simon) has told in detail what God did when he first began to show his concern for taking from among the Goyim (Gentiles) a people to bear his name. And the words of the Prophets are in complete harmony with this for it is written, "After this, I will return; and I will rebuild the fallen tent of David. I will rebuild its ruins, I will restore it, so that the rest of mankind may seek the Lord, that is, all the Goyim who have been called by my name," says ADONAI, who is doing these things. All this has been known for ages.'" CJB

Acts 15:19-21 "'Therefore, my opinion is that we should not put obstacles in the way of the Goyim who are turning to God. Instead, we should write them a letter telling them to abstain from things polluted by idols, from fornication, from what is strangled and from blood. For from the earliest times, Moshe (Moses) has had in every city those who proclaim him, with his words being read in the synagogues every Shabbat.'" CJB

Romans 1:5-6 "Through him we received grace and were given the work of being an emissary on his behalf promoting trust-grounded obedience among all the Gentiles, including you, who have been called by Yeshua the Messiah." CJB

Romans 11:11 " 'In that case, I say, isn't it that they have stumbled with the result that they have permanently fallen away?' Heaven forbid! Quite the contrary, it is by means of their stumbling that the deliverance has come to the Gentiles, in order to provoke them to jealousy." CJB

<u>*Romans 15:9-12*</u> *"... and in order to show his mercy by causing the Gentiles to glorify God—as it is written in the Tanakh (Old Testament) 'Because of this I will acknowledge you among the Gentiles and sing praise to your name.' And again it says, 'Gentiles, rejoice with his people.' And again, 'Praise ADONAI, all Gentiles! Let all peoples praise him!' And again, Yesha'yahu (Isaiah) says, 'The root of Yishai (Jesse) will come, he who arises to rule Gentiles; Gentiles will put their hope in him.'" CJB*

<u>*Romans 15:16*</u> *"... to be a servant of the Messiah Yeshua for the Gentiles, with the priestly duty of presenting the Good News of God, so that the Gentiles may be an acceptable offering, made holy by the Ruach HaKodesh." CJB*

<u>*Romans 15:27*</u> *"They were pleased to do it, but the fact is that they owe it to them. For if the Gentiles have shared with the Jews in spiritual matters, then the Gentiles clearly have a duty to help the Jews in material matters." CJB*

<u>*Ephesians 2:11*</u> *"Therefore, remember your former state: you Gentiles by birth—called the Uncircumcised by those who, merely because of an operation on their flesh, are called the Circumcised—at that time had no Messiah." CJB*

<u>*Ephesians 3:6*</u> *"... that in union with the Messiah and through the Good News the Gentiles were to be joint heirs, a joint body and joint sharers with the Jews in what God has promised." CJB*

Prayer of Revelation:

Abba, Father,

As we have read a story about a woman named Lydia who, as a Gentile, searched for a true Savior and found Yeshua as her saving grace, may we become willing to change from our pagan ways and follow the Jewish Messiah, Yeshua, with all our hearts. May we become honest before You and tell You that to leave the ways we have been taught in the church and to pick up Your celebrations of worship will be hard. So many of us have put our families first, our reputations in the community first, and we have compromised with Your Holy Word. Please forgive us. We ask for the eyes of our hearts to be opened, as Lydia's eyes were opened, to walk in the truth. We ask for grace and compassion for those that will not understand our choices for this time. We ask, Ruach HaKodesh, that You will teach us and guide us into all truth so that we will be found on the path of truth and not lost to deception and ignorance. We thank You for Your Word which is set before us to find the hidden treasures within. Give us endurance and perseverance to gain the crown of victory.

In Yeshua's Name.

Amen

Glossary of Hebrew Words

Abraham, Isaac, Jacob	-	Patriarchs of Israel. Physical and spiritual ancestors of Judaism
Adonai	-	Lord
Aleph & Tav	-	First and last letters of the Hebrew alphabet
Anti-Semitic	-	Prejudice against or hostility toward Jews as a group
Aramaic	-	Native language of Jesus
B'rit Hadashah	-	New Testament
B'Shem	-	"In The Name"
Bereans	-	Examined the scriptures daily to see if what Paul said was true
Bethlehem	-	House of Bread
Bridal Contract	-	"Ketubah" Jewish marriage agreement to protect and provide for the wife
Brit	-	Circumcision ceremony
Caleb & Joshua	-	2 of the spies Moses sent to spy out the land of Canaan
Challah	-	Special braided bread eaten by Jews on the Sabbath and holidays
Chuppah	-	Wedding canopy

Covenant	-	A solemn promise made by one person to do or not do something specific
Doda	-	Aunt
Feasts of the Lord	-	7 yearly feasts appointed by the Lord, to be observed by Israel
Galilee	-	Region in Northern Israel / Sea of Galilee
Gentiles/Goyim	-	Non-Jews
Ha Mashiach	-	The Messiah (The Christ/Savior)
Hallel	-	A Jewish prayer consisting of 6 Psalms recited on Jewish holidays
HaShem	-	Hebrew for "The Name", referring to God
Herod	-	King of Judea at the time of Jesus
Holy of Holies	-	The inner sanctuary of the Tabernacle and later the Temple
Jaffa Gate	-	One of the Gates into the Old City of Jerusalem
Judah	-	A son of Jacob, one of the 12 Tribes of Israel
Kefa	-	Peter
Kosher	-	Food in accord with the Jewish dietary laws
Lamb's Book of Life	-	The book containing the names of those saved by the blood of the Lamb
Levitical Law	-	Legal and priestly rules set out in the 3rd book of the Torah, Leviticus
Manna	-	The food that God miraculously provided to the Israelites in the desert

Matzah	-	An unleavened bread, the official food of Passover
Menorah	-	7-branched candelabrum used in the Temple, symbol of Judaism/Israel
Messianic Gentiles	-	Non-Jews who believe Jesus (Yeshua) is the Jewish Messiah
Mezuzzah	-	A cylinder containing scripture affixed to the doorposts of Jewish homes
Minyan	-	A group of ten men, the number required for religious meetings, prayer
Mitzvot	-	Acts of kindness, based on the commandments in the Torah
Moabite	-	Inhabitant of Moab – modern day Jordan
Moshe	-	Moses
Mount Sinai	-	Mountain where God gave the law to the Israelites
Mt. Moriah	-	The Temple Mount in Jerusalem/Also where Abraham sacrificed Isaac
Myrrh	-	Spice
Na'aseh V'nishma	-	"We will obey and then understand"
New Moon	-	The first visible crescent of the moon
Passover Lamb	-	The Lamb that was sacrificed on the night of the Exodus from Egypt / Jesus
Passover Seder	-	Jewish ritual feast commemorating the Exodus from Egypt

Pesach	-	Passover
Pharaoh	-	Ancient Egyptian King
Pharisees	-	A Jewish sect during the Second Temple period
Promised Land	-	The Land of Israel, which was promised by God to Abraham's descendants
Prophetess	-	A female prophet
Rabbi	-	Teacher
Renewed Testament	-	The New Testament or B'rit Hadashah
Rosh Hashanah	-	Jewish New Year
Ruach HaKodesh	-	Holy Spirit
Sadducees	-	Jewish sect during the Second Temple period
Sages	-	The Rabbis of the Mishnah and Talmud
Sanhedrin	-	Assembly of judges in ancient Israel
Scribe	-	One who copied sacred text by hand
Shabbat Shalom	-	"Sabbath Peace", a greeting used on the Sabbath
Shabbat	-	Sabbath
Shalom	-	Peace
Sheep's Gate	-	One of the Gates into the Old City of Jerusalem
Shekels	-	The currency of Israel
Shekinah	-	God's presence
Shema	-	From Deuteronomy, "Hear O Israel, the Lord our God, the Lord is One".

Shaddai	-	A Judaic name of God meaning "God Almighty who is all sufficient"
Shofar	-	Ram's Horn
Shuk	-	Open marketplace
Simchah Torah	-	"Rejoice in the Word", celebration at the end of the Feast of Tabernacles
Solomon's Temple	-	The first Jewish Temple, built by King Solomon
Songs of Ascent	-	Psalms 120-134, sung as the Jews would "Go up" to Jerusalem to worship
Synagogue	-	Jewish place of worship
T'shuvah	-	Turn around, repent
Tallit	-	Prayer shawl
Talmid	-	Student
Tanakh	-	Old Testament
Tear Bottle	-	Bottle containing the tears of those whose loved ones went to war
Temple Mount	-	Mountain where the First and Second Jewish Temples were located
Temple	-	Holy Temple of God in Jerusalem
Torah	-	First 5 books of the Bible – Books of Moses
Tribes	-	12 Tribes of Israel, named for Jacob's 12 sons
Y'hoshua	-	Joshua
Ya'akov	-	Jacob
Yahweh	-	The Name of the God of Israel

Yeshua	-	Jesus
Yom Rishon	-	First day of the week
Yom Shi Shi	-	Sixth day of the week
Zion	-	Land of Israel and its capitol, Jerusalem. A specific mountain in Jerusalem.

Made in the USA
Columbia, SC
26 June 2024

37539715R00095